SH●RK ASSAULT

AN AMAZING STORY OF SURVIVAL

Peter Jennings and Nicole Moore

SH RK ASSAULT

AN AMAZING STORY OF SURVIVAL

DUNDURN
TORONTO

Design: Janette Thompson (Jansom)
Cover Design: Laura Boyle
Cover Image: Timothy Fraser, timfraser.com. Shark: Richard Brooks/iStock.com
Printer: Webcom

Library and Archives Canada Cataloguing in Publication

Jennings, Peter, 1948-, author
    Shark assault : an amazing story of survival / Peter Jennings and Nicole Moore.

Issued in print and electronic formats.
ISBN 978-1-4597-3217-9 (paperback).--ISBN 978-1-4597-3218-6 (pdf).--ISBN 978-1-4597-3219-3 (epub)

    1. Moore, Nicole, 1972-. 2. Shark attacks--Mexico. 3. Tourists--Mexico--Biography. 4. Amputees--Rehabilitation--Canada--Biography. 5. Nurses--Canada--Biography. I. Moore, Nicole, 1972-, author II. Title.

QL638.9.J45 2015   597.3   C2015-902840-X
                                         C2015-902841-8

1 2 3 4 5   19 18 17 16 15

  Canadä

We acknowledge the support of the **Canada Council for the Arts** and the **Ontario Arts Council** for our publishing program. We also acknowledge the financial support of the **Government of Canada** through the **Canada Book Fund** and **Livres Canada Books**, and the **Government of Ontario** through the **Ontario Book Publishing Tax Credit** and the **Ontario Media Development Corporation**.

Care has been taken to trace the ownership of copyright material used in this book. The author and the publisher welcome any information enabling them to rectify any references or credits in subsequent editions.

— *J. Kirk Howard, President*

The publisher is not responsible for websites or their content unless they are owned by the publisher.

Printed and bound in Canada.

VISIT US AT
Dundurn.com | @dundurnpress | Facebook.com/dundurnpress | Pinterest.com/dundurnpress

Dundurn
3 Church Street, Suite 500
Toronto, Ontario, Canada
M5E 1M2

It's a wilderness experience when we enter the sea and we as humans do not have a guarantee when we go there.

— George H. Burgess, Director, Florida Program for Shark Research and International Shark Attack File

———◆———

The last word in ignorance is the man who says of an animal or plant, "What good is it?"

— Aldo Leopold (1887–1948), ecologist and environmentalist

———◆———

The word I would use to describe Nicole is tenacious: *"I'm going to do it, damn it, I'm going to plug through no matter what, just watch me!" That's how she handles her life.*

— Toni Amadei, Nicole's travel mate on the trip to Cancún

———◆———

It is rare to see someone experience the trauma of so many surgeries yet be so strong, positive, and full of hope as Nicole Moore. She is an inspiration.

— Dr. Laura Snell, Division of Plastic and Reconstructive Surgery, Sunnybrook Health Sciences Centre, Toronto

———◆———

Caring can move mountains. Without a sense of care, there is no community.

— Nicole Moore

Contents

INTRODUCTION

Can There Be a Greater Fear?

One of the most dreadful torments of the human imagination is fear of a shark attack. Even your worst nightmare can't compare to the reality.

Imagine being rendered nearly helpless as a massive, primitive killing machine beats at you, tearing at your flesh with unbelievable savagery. Your skin is ripped open and you hear the cracking of your bones. You are helpless and horrified as your organs are devoured with ease.

A bull shark.

Jose Angel Astor

Huge, indifferent, razor-edged teeth — grown for the sole purpose of hacking away at anything the shark senses is food or foe — gnash at your body, leaving you dying in a sea of blood.

For Nicole Moore, a thirty-nine-year-old nurse from Orangeville, Ontario, such a horrifying agony is not just imagined. It is how her life was assaulted.

This is her story.

1

Emergency in Mexico

She stands on the quiet sands at the Cancún resort, staring out at a calm ocean of turquoise beauty. Her mind darts back to months earlier when events on this same beach changed her life in a way few people would have the courage to confront, let alone survive. Even she wonders how she's pulled through.

The beach is eerily silent. The hush is somewhat overwhelming, a bit sinister.

Is the quiet because it's off-season, with fewer people enjoying the posh vacation destination? Or do the few guests know of her circumstances? Perhaps they are keeping their distance, allowing her time and solitude, out of respect.

Soon the camera crew that has followed her out of Toronto to Mexico — *uninvited* — will be there to record the compulsion she feels she cannot avoid: facing her fears head on. Nicole Moore is determined to step into the Caribbean Sea at the exact spot where she was attacked months before. She will master the influence that has become the ruler of her existence.

But the silence is undermining her resolve.

A small silver fish suddenly breaks the shallow surface, the unexpected splash causing her neck to jerk back. Off in the distance she hears the muffled howl of a siren. She blinks her eyes, shaking her head to banish the memory of the fateful ambulance ride that only months ago was truly a race against time. That very phrase can be a little over the top, but in the case of Nicole Moore being rushed to Hospiten Cancún on the afternoon of January 31, 2011, nothing could have been closer to the truth. She was as near to death as anyone could be. Minutes — seconds — mattered.

Her body scarred and deformed, missing her left arm and much of her left leg muscles — painful realities she is forced to endure every waking moment — Nicole shuts her eyes. Her mind summons up that earth-shattering day where she had to cope with a treacherous ambulance journey, strapped to a backboard that was not well secured, flapping about as the inexperienced driver tackled the mounting bumps in the road, while paramedics struggled to find any blood pressure reading at all. This was the point when Nicole realized she had probably reached the end of her life. She was racing to the hospital less and less as a survivor, more and more as a fatality.

Her memories take over. She is propelled back to feeling the fear in her gut, the helplessness, and especially the frustration of that terrible day. She begins reliving the experience of horror in a surreal manner. She's back in the ambulance. She's being hurled about. She's recognizing that her body has started to shut down peripherally. She's already lost 60 percent of her blood. Her skin is ashen grey. Circulation has slowed to her legs, arms, and hands, and her organs are shutting down. She fights for each gasp of air; there isn't enough blood left to make her lungs do their job. And she knows that in the fifty minutes since she's been attacked and severely wounded, little anyone has done has seemed to help.

As an experienced nurse, Nicole knows her situation is bad. Really bad. She understands she has mere minutes left in her life. Only her heart and brain are functioning now, and they are down for the count. Once her heart checks out she'll have maybe two minutes before brain damage sets in.

And then death.

At home they'd call her condition "critical, life threatening."

Still, the young ambulance driver comes through, making it to the hospital, where staff members whisk her inside and plant her on a trauma bed. But nothing will be simple. Already there is a problem: they've never dealt with this kind of attack before. They seem unsure of what to do. Nicole panics because she fears for her life, while the people around her seem more focused on whether she has adequate insurance coverage. They ramble on in Spanish about her capacity to pay for what they are unsure they will do in the first place.

"Where and what is her insurance situation?" one administrator asks.

"Who is going to pay for her treatment?" another demands.

Finally an on-duty doctor arrives. "We need to do something now!" he commands in English. And the medical staff members go into action, for which Nicole gasps her heartfelt thanks.

The doctors determine one thing: they cannot put in an IV because Nicole's body has already experienced so much trauma that her system has given out, denying blood to her major organs. Her veins continue to empty as her circulation decreases. They are afraid that not enough blood is getting to her brain, so they make a snap decision to insert a central line directly into her heart. It is an urgent attempt to keep Nicole alive.

They use a subclavian approach in her right shoulder to try to access the aorta. This is a complex procedure with the potential for life-threatening complications; the lung can easily be nicked making it difficult for the patient to breathe. Unfortunately, the approach doesn't go well and the team isn't able to insert the central line on the first try. Despite their best efforts, Nicole Moore is dying. The clock is ticking, but the medical team still can't insert the central line. Seemingly in desperation they tell her: "We are now going to put you to sleep."

She's frightened because she can no longer breathe.

But we're getting ahead of ourselves. How did Nicole Moore end up fighting for her life in a Mexican hospital?

2

There's Moore to Life

Nicole is the kind of person who thoroughly engages in a conversation. Her eyes track yours, revealing an inner confidence. She is articulate and doesn't shy away from providing details. Her voice is soft and reassuring, her well-chosen words reveal an educated command of the language. In conversation she may seem a bit hesitant at first, like she's waiting to see

Nicole today.

what the dimensions of the exchange will be, but once you've overcome any doubt on her part you're as welcome as a family member.

She was born in 1972 in London, Ontario, the only child of Monica Rogers and Alberto Baldassari. Monica hailed from Ireland, but was orphaned and adopted by an affluent American family who raised her in the United States. Alberto is from Pistoia, Italy, born in the midst of the Second World War and brought up in very hard post-war conditions — an environment so difficult that he had to mature quickly. Alberto left home at a young age to find work.

He was in the U.S. attending a training course when he met Monica. She was recently widowed and had a young daughter, named Angela. In Alberto's words, "She was definitely a beautiful woman with a lovely, warm personality to match. Fortunately, it didn't take long for the attraction to be mutual. I left my family, friends and everything I had ever known in Italy and moved permanently to North America for love."

They married in the States, but fate brought them to Canada, where Nicole was born.

Nicole seems to have borrowed the fine qualities of both her parents. From her mom came her beauty, her nurturing side, her caring, her fondness for animals, her love for people, and need to give back to

Personal Collection of Nicole Moore

Nicole's mother, Monica Rogers.

her community. From her dad she inherited strength, independence, appreciation for fitness, and a drive to be healthy. Alberto also gave his daughter her sense of security, and the knowledge that she is loved and valued. Nicole jokes that she got his expensive tastes too.

"He's a very logical person," she says. "If there's a problem, fix it and move on. Everything else in my personality comes from me: being positive, not being bitter and negative, not letting the world beat me down ... I don't know where that came from, but that's just me." Good thing, too, because life was soon going to challenge Nicole in ways that no one should have to experience.

Monica was loving and presented a wonderful side to her children, but she suffered from schizophrenia. She managed to deal with this for years, but eventually the condition began to manifest itself in many dark ways that caused problems for the family.

Eventually it became evident that Alberto and Monica's marriage was not destined to last. As they separated the couple debated the best outcome. Eventually they agreed that Nicole would live with her dad, while her half-sister, Angela, went with their mom and grandparents. "As I'm

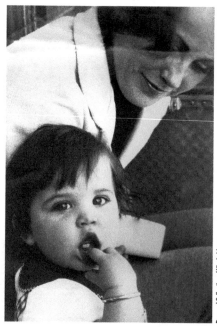

Alberto and Monica, young and happy together.

Baby Nicole and her mom.

Personal Collection of Nicole Moore

sure others can attest, it's tough growing up with a parent suffering from mental illness," Nicole says as she reflects back to that time. "I was able to spend time with my mother and sister occasionally, and I did discover awareness and learning from my mom's incredible qualities. But unfortunately, my sister and I saw the effects of this awful disease too. My mother's coping mechanisms included seeking out physically abusive relationships, suicidal tendencies, and alcoholism. A child should never, ever watch their parent being beaten much less find them in a pool of their own blood from a suicide attempt. It changes a child's innocence forever."

Alberto sought to lessen the impact by raising Nicole in a stable and disciplined environment, acting as a role model in her younger years and as a caring, affectionate friend later on, contributing to her stamina, seeing her become more independent, more of a fighter. A survivor. These were qualities that would stand her in good stead down the road — qualities that would help save her life.

Because Alberto's job involved a lot of travel, Nicole was often left with a babysitter. "It seemed like I was with someone else's family more often than I was at home with my dad," she explains. "When my father wasn't travelling for work, he travelled for pleasure, something that rarely included me. I understood even back then that downtime was important for him, and I knew it must've been hard being a single parent, especially for an Italian man who was raised with the mentality that child rearing was more of a mother's role than a father's. But when he didn't include me on his vacations, it made me bitter and left me feeling like I didn't fit in anywhere. In the end, I guess it served a purpose, teaching me how to be independent and how to fight my own battles."

Alberto did include his daughter on his trips back home to Italy every few years, which became a part of Nicole's upbringing. He stressed the importance of worldliness and family values, as well as the benefits of being exposed to other cultures. Her grandparents, aunts, and uncles in Italy opened her eyes to life beyond North America, contributing to the breadth of her character development. Nicole became more open minded, accepting of other views, more liberal.

When she was seven, Nicole fell in love with dance. Within a few years she lived and breathed ballet. As high school approached, she decided she wanted to attend a school of the arts. But she wasn't sure if she was talented enough. The auditions were nerve-racking, and waiting to hear back was painful. The stress was worth it, however, when she finally got her acceptance letter.

Nicole was an energetic girl with a habit of taking things to the limit, so she was determined to excel. Dance is really demanding. You're on your feet for long periods of time, putting your body through great strain. Nicole was doing ballet, modern, acro, jazz, even African dance, five days a week, sometimes twice a day. And this was on top of the numerous athletics she was into as well.

"My body couldn't handle it," she recalls, "and I hurt my back pretty seriously. They told me I had to stop or I wouldn't be walking, it was that bad. So I had no choice. At sixteen I quit dance. It was a pretty sad decision, because this was such a part of my life! I wanted *so* much to be a dancer. I was devastated."

The void that quitting dancing left in her life was compounded by the discovery that Nicole had basal cell carcinoma. The growth was smack in the middle of her face, under the skin beside her nose. It wasn't really noticeable and grew for years until it finally became symptomatic. She learned she would need multiple operations to remove it.

Of course, teenagers are consumed with their looks, and being told that her face might be disfigured for some time was upsetting. Nicole hit a wall. "No dancing! And now I'm going to be ugly … life is over!"

The operating doctors told her they weren't sure if the tumour had reached bone. If it had that would make it malignant. Nicole came to understand that the situation could be a lot worse than having a scar on her face. So at age sixteen she underwent surgery for the first time in her young life. The good news was that the tumour was benign and removed entirely, but her face being disfigured for months was tough. Thinking back to that time, Nicole says softly, almost to herself, "I learned how cruel kids could be."

During that same year, Nicole took a trip to Italy. Lacking a motherly influence at home, she'd never mastered the art of pretty hair or makeup like the other girls. Instead, she chose to direct her attention to boys, cool clothes, and ballet. But a close family friend who ran an Italian beauty salon, Deanna Carletti, encouraged her to take advantage of her natural good looks.

Deanna worked her magic on Nicole, styling her hair attractively. It was a total revelation to the young girl. She took one look in the mirror and decided that she could see what others had been telling her: with or without a scar running down the middle of her face, she was attractive. She could work with this. And it was the right time: on her return to Canada, it would be high school, boys, parties … "Let's face it, the hunky guys you want to be with don't always set out to date sports-crazed tomboys. It was a good time for a change."

Life moved on. Where dance had occupied her, sports became the new outlet. Any sport. And she started scuba diving too. Underwater, Nicole was constantly aware of her surroundings, realizing there could always be some form of threat nearby. She was careful. But she never thought she'd be attacked by a shark. Ironically she once swam with sharks and fed them with her left hand, the one that would be amputated years later.

Volleyball became another passion. The sport was her hands-down favourite, virtually dominating her life: playing, coaching, on the beach circuit … she lived and breathed volleyball. Sadly, this natural zest for competition and physical activity was what put her on a beach in Mexico years later — the place where she would face horrific, life-changing trauma.

School could be a trial for Nicole. Certain aspects seemed more challenging for her than for her friends. Testing determined that she was dyslexic, which was causing her difficulty in reading and comprehension accuracy. Nicole confronted the diagnosis with her characteristic composure. She decided that it might take her a little longer to read, write, or spell, but when she did those things they would be done flawlessly. And as a self-confessed control freak, this fell in line with her overall approach to life: do it right, do it well, keep moving forward.

As if her childhood was not demanding enough, a shocking series of events threatened her sanity, stability, and self-respect, burdening her in a way that no child should be. Starting when she was just seven and continuing well into her ninth year, a family acquaintance advanced on her in secret and forced her to perform sexual acts.

If the fates had decided that Nicole's existence was to be challenging (and the toll was mounting, based on her parents' separation, her mother's illness, basal cell carcinoma, having her love of dancing jerked away from her, grappling with dyslexia), this was the meanest strain of all. The abuse was drawn out, and while these offences did unhinge young Nicole for some time, her resolute strength and ability to persevere eventually allowed her to deal with this assault. She compartmentalized it and continued facing the world with her characteristic optimism and buoyancy, albeit never forgetting how slender one's grip on life can be.

"There's no question I had to confront way too many demons." Nicole's voice softens when she says that, her body sagging slightly as she considers the weight of those burdens. "Most people are unaware of the trials I endured as a kid because I simply don't talk about that time. And I certainly don't intend to dwell on it now. It's in the past and that's where it stays. But I will say this: if I can summon up the internal strength to persist and come out a winner in the end, then others can too. That's my message.

"That I have survived is a result of recognizing and accepting that the world has its share of evil. There is much out there that can so easily send you spiralling out of control. But you know what: there's much more joy to life than unpleasantness. I've been graced with an inner resolve that helps add a rudder to my being. For the most part I've been able to put aside the negative forces that could have derailed me and focus on all the outstanding advantages offered to me. They say adversity makes you stronger. Hey! I'm the poster girl for that expression!"

Keep Moving Forward.

Nicole entered college, where she took arts with a minor in sports medicine, and eventually became a personal trainer.

In 1996 Nicole's mother passed away. She was fifty. Nicole was twenty-three. "It changes you," Nicole reflects quietly. "When someone you're close to dies, you're left picking up the pieces of your life. You find yourself needing to redefine things, make adjustments, learn how to carry on in a different environment ... regroup, change priorities. I suppose my mom's death made me stronger ... but, you know, there are better ways to achieve that strength."

Nicole had cared for her mother during the final stages of her illness. In doing so she experienced a health system that failed to deliver palliative care well, and she became passionate about that. In fact, it changed the direction of her life. She decided then and there that joining the medical profession would allow her to turn her passion for helping others into a job where she could look after people who were in pain or dying. She found her calling in nursing.

Following her training she simply fell in love with the profession. Being able to help people face physical challenges was the perfect way for Nicole to channel her desire to give back, to help, something that's been a constant throughout her life. Nursing and Nicole were made for each other.

As she talks about this time in her life, Nicole pauses, looking down, a tinge of sadness in her pretty hazel eyes. This is not an emotion she often reveals. "You know, I *loved* nursing," she offers in a soft voice. "It was so fulfilling. I was a happy nurse. I loved the interaction with people. I can honestly say I was good at what I did. I'd find occasions to interact with patients even if it was during my own time off. To comfort them.... I really felt I was helping them with whatever they were going through. I liked the challenge as well. I'm a trauma junkie so I really love the adrenalin. Now, though, so much of that has to be part of my past since I can no longer practise as a nurse."

In 1998 Nicole met Jason Moore. She was smitten when she came upon him in the college halls. It was love at first sight. When she discovered he was going on a skiing outing, Nicole, being an avid downhill skier, thought she could impress Jay and get his attention. She signed up for the same trip.

Born in a small farming community in northern Ontario, Jay had come south to study law enforcement, ending up by chance at the same college where Nicole was studying nursing. A handsome young man with a love of athletics, he admits to having been shy and a bit naive at the time.

"You know, back then," Jay recollects, "I never noticed Nicole trying to catch my attention. I thought she was gorgeous, but I didn't think there was any way she'd be interested in me. But when we met up later that night at an after-ski party we talked together to well past midnight. I knew I had to see her again."

Their first date was less than promising. Jay had decided on dinner and a movie. When Nicole went to meet him at school he'd just finished some sports activity, and she had to stand around waiting while he got ready. "As if that wasn't enough," he recalls, "being the romantic guy I am (not!), I took her to a sports bar. And then when I went to pay with my debit card it turned out they didn't even take debit cards, so I had to make Nicole pay. Not good! Next we went to the movie. I had chosen *Titanic*, a three-hour epic. Being a farm boy, I'm used to getting up early, but that means I'm in bed before ten … I fell asleep before the iceberg was even a rumour. Nicole woke me while wiping the drool off her shoulder and suggested we leave. Definitely not a great beginning to a new relationship!"

Still, that wasn't about to get in the way of their keenness for another date.

In 2002 Nicole Baldassari and Jason Moore were married.

Thinking back to the wedding, Nicole enthusiastically exclaims: "Listen to this. Jay and I never knew this about each other until, literally, our wedding day. The day I met this wonderful, unassuming, handsome guy — even after that nightmare first date — I went home and wrote in

Nicole and Jason on their wedding day.

my daily journal that I'd met the man I was going to marry. I just *knew* it! I'd never been more certain of anything. But — and this is pretty karma-like — after that first date Jay called his mother and told her, 'I just met the girl I'm going to marry.' Can you believe that? Some things are just meant to be."

Since Nicole had been living with her father for some time, Jay simply moved in with them. The trio got along well. There was mutual respect between father-in-law and son-in-law.

"It's a European thing, I admit," explains Alberto. "There, families living together is the norm. Not so much here, but it worked for us. Still does."

Indeed, Alberto — now retired from a career in information technology — lives in a separate apartment within the sprawling Moore house in Orangeville, a picturesque town of 28,000 located an hour northwest of Toronto. Nicole and Jay agree it's a nice arrangement, which includes their two delightful daughters Tia (age seven when the shark attack happened) and Ella (who was six at the time), and, of course, Marley the puppy.

That move to Orangeville was beneficial all around. Nicole quickly assumed a nursing position with the Headwaters Health Care Centre and Jay was hired by the town's police service. The community welcomed the friendly couple and their kids. Life was good.

3

The Great Mexicali Adventure

Cancún is in the Mexican state of Quintana Roo, located in the Yucatán Peninsula. The world-renowned tourist destination comprises the Mayan Riviera, featuring miles of powdery sand beaches, crystal-clear waters, magnificent historical sites, and welcoming Mexican hospitality, all of which lures winter-weary travellers from the north with open arms. To

The beautiful blue waters of Cancún.

Nicole Moore and a zestful group of nine friends, Cancún seemed like a sublime idea.

The plan started with Terri Holden, a long-time resident of Orangeville whose exercise classes were the common bond of the Cancún adventurers. Terri had established a personal-training business many years previously and some of the ladies had been coming to her classes for fifteen years or more. Ken had been going for almost twenty years.

Ken Mihan was unquestionably the odd man out in the group of nine women. He's an Air Canada pilot who has a lot of time off, and he likes to keep fit. He had started exercising with Terri back in 1991 and was the only guy there, but that was okay.

Terri's fiftieth birthday was coming up, and since she had played a series of practical jokes on various pals who'd already turned fifty she wanted to get out of town before any of them could taking revenge.

For Donna Holwell, one of Terri's oldest friends, Cancún was going to be a special treat. She had been enduring cancer treatments for a particularly aggressive form of the disease. But she was in remission and ready to celebrate. No more chemo, no more radiation!

The Cancún planning committee.

Toni Amadie, a long-time member of the exercise clan (and a woman Nicole calls "In a league of her own … I can honestly say that I have never met, nor will I meet, a better person than her"), felt that after talking about the trip for almost two years it was time to make a decision. Her feeling was that Terri's fiftieth birthday and her thirtieth year of being an instructor, and Ken's and the original group's twentieth year, represented a series of milestones. Definitely good reasons to go away and celebrate.

Kathy Sutton, a travel agent and member of the class, had been to Cancún before. She felt certain the area provided a great place to unwind and the Grand Park Royal Cancún Caribe hotel offered good value for the group. "I recall we considered some other locales but the Grand Park seemed to make the most sense," says Sandra Schad, another eager participant. "The best facilities at the best price point. Didn't take much to convince me to go!"

As a pilot, Ken had been to Cancún several times. He'd enjoyed swimming in the Caribbean regularly. "You know, on all of the occasions I've swum at Cancún's beaches — or at any other beach for that matter — I never gave the first thought to sharks," Ken says wistfully. "Just took it for granted I could swim there. Just like Nicole felt on that day…."

One of Terri's criteria for the trip was a great beach for walking. The group members knew that if they were travelling with her there was bound to be a certain amount of fitness involved. And the beaches in Cancún are fabulous for walks. Terri's aim was to get the gang out there every day, pounding the sand.

"We agreed to meet Terri's beach-walking routine," laughs Donna. "But no push ups or anything like that. I mean, c'mon, this is a vacation we're talking about!"

Nicole was the baby of the group. Most of her classmates were in their late forties, early fifties. She was the newbie, still in her thirties, and had joined less than a year before. She was just getting to know the long-term members when the notion of the trip came up. Ready to take a brief break from her busy activities as nurse, wife, mom, and daughter, she readily agreed to join in.

Jay was onside with the idea of his wife's upcoming escapade. When he and Nicole had first come together, he had debts, no assets, maybe a set of sheets and a couple of towels. Nicole supported them, paying for everything they needed. So when she brought up the trip his reaction was, "Hey, it's your turn. Go have some fun."

"Terri would have people up to her cottage at the end of the season," says Cyndi Cramer, another group member, "but this was so special for us to travel to Mexico together. It was a pretty big to-do. Our expectations for fun were high."

And so the plan was set. In January 2011 the Great Mexicali Adventure would unfold.

The friends left Toronto at 6:30 a.m. on Thursday, January 27, 2011, and the plane touched down four hours later.

When they arrived the hotel did not have their rooms ready, so they ventured outside to hang by the pool and catch some rays. But it quickly became clear that all they were going to catch was a cold! Cancún was experiencing unnaturally cool weather. Someone has a photo of all of them shivering in windbreakers, huddling out of the wind. Fortunately, the weather gods stepped in and the warm climate for which the Caribbean coast of Mexico is famous returned.

Everyone agreed that once they settled in, it was a fantastic trip. Whether they were getting active or lolling on a recliner with a good book, Cancún seemed to meet their needs.

"I just love these girls," Nicole says about the exercise group. "Their quality, their caring, their good sense of humour ... they're just wonderful people I really enjoy being with. You know, you need to surround yourself with the ones who make you feel good."

Ken felt a little strange about being the only guy on a trip with nine women, but he'd been friends with Terri for twenty years and, in his own words, "She sure as hell wasn't going to celebrate her fiftieth without me being there! Plus, I knew most of these ladies really well from the exercise classes."

After a few days all the people who worked at the resort were calling out to Ken, "Hey, Superman!" The ladies started referring to themselves as his "chicas."

"People kept asking Ken, 'Are you married to any of these women?'" Cyndi explains. "Ken would say, 'Nope.' So they'd ask, 'Well, how did

Superman and the chicas.

Nicole with the band at the Grand Park Royal Cancún Caribe.

you get to be here with them?' and he'd reply, 'Just lucky I guess.' And that's when they started with the Superman stuff."

Several of the group had no interest in swimming in the ocean — in retrospect, maybe they were the smart ones — but others would play volleyball and the first thing they'd do afterward is hit the surf to wash away all the sand picked up in the game. "R 'n R in the sun was my goal," says Kathy. "But most of us didn't have Nicole's energy ... I'll walk in the ocean but I never swim in it. Especially now."

"I've swum in the ocean at other places," explains Sandra, "but it's funny, I didn't in Cancún. Don't know why. Honestly, I wasn't thinking about sharks or anything...."

Relaxation dominated this Mexican escape. Even on Terri's birthday, the group ordered a massage for her in the afternoon and then everyone got dolled up to paint the town after dinner, but the sun, exercise, drinks, and food took their toll. The gang threw in the towel, saying, "Tomorrow night for sure," before heading off to bed.

4

Point of No Return

January 31, 2011. Day four of the vacation adventure.

Ten years earlier, a bull shark, known for its aggressive nature and preference for shallow, warm water, was born in an estuary of the Reserva Natural Tres Rios, Mexico, part of a litter of eight. It arrived free-swimming, already more than two feet long.

The bull shark is considered by many experts the most dangerous shark in the world. Of the 440 species of sharks, they are thought to be the most aggressive and very nasty.

Having left its estuary birthplace, the seven-foot-long, grey, barrel-shaped bull shark migrated up the coast of Mexico. The bull's small eyes and their placement on its head render the animal sight-disadvantaged compared to other sharks. Hence its innate hunting strategy, known as bump and bite: the shark butts the intended prey with its blunt head. That bump is investigative, helping determine just what it's about to chomp on, and then the animal sinks its teeth into the flesh to sample the meal.

Bulls are known for their agility and quick bursts of speed. No other ocean animal threatens it. This beast has the strongest bite of any shark species: a steel-trap-like bite force of up to thirteen hundred pounds per square inch, the highest among all investigated cartilaginous fishes. And it has a mouthful of hundreds of wide, long triangular teeth with ser-rated edges, ideal tools for ripping apart the flesh of its prey.

Nathan Cierzynski

A bull shark.

In murky, shallow water, the bull shark may be fooled into thinking someone splashing around is a tasty fish in trouble. Its attack behaviour is to hit a target, circle, hit again, and repeat. Little will get in this shark's way when it's on a mission.

Almost all marine experts agree that the danger presented by sharks has been exaggerated. The fact remains that there are way more annual fatalities from lightning strikes than shark attacks. But on this day when the life of a young, Canadian nurse enjoying the warm waters of Cancún will be invaded and altered forever, statistics don't matter.

And here's one more detail worth knowing: a recent hurricane had washed out many Cancún beaches, altering the habitat where sharks congregate. The creatures of the sea were left disoriented and defensive. Experts tell us that when a shark is acting that way, look out!*

---

*The authors acknowledge with thanks the insights of shark attack expert George H. Burgess, director, Florida Program for Shark Research and International Shark Attack File, and Dr. Gregory Skomal, senior biologist at the Massachusetts Division of Marine Fisheries, author of *The Shark Handbook*, and one of the world's leading shark experts. They have provided details on the likely course of events that led to the attack on Nicole Moore.

5

Shark Attack

There is not one chance in millions that the events you are going to read about *should* have occurred. Statistically, that's how slim the chances were of a bull shark attacking Nicole Moore in waist-deep water on that dreadful day. Not only that, but given the seriousness of the wounds she incurred Nicole should not have survived.

Instead, quite amazingly, she was handed a fighting chance to rediscover the joy in her life.

"On that day, my whole existence changed in a matter of seconds," Nicole explains. "Makes you feel like you're very out of control."

That's putting it mildly.

"It haunts me to this day," says Nicole's friend Terri Holden. She's a strong woman, no stranger to trauma, having experienced the anguish of her husband's death from a gruesome accident nearly thirty years ago. But Terri is resilient, the result of a positive mental attitude and her many years of fitness training. Still, as she talks about Cancún her tears flow. "I can't get over the fact I'm responsible for this," she says, visibly upset more than two years later. "I encouraged Nicole to join our group. I persuaded her to come on the trip to Mexico. If I hadn't done that, this awful attack would never have taken place."

But no one could have predicted such a horrific event.

Monday, January 31, 2011

While several of her friends head into town to explore shopping opportunities, Nicole indulges her love of volleyball with a morning game on the beach. Her team is winning when she begs off, needing to get ready for a noon scuba diving jaunt she's agreed to join. But first, she'll hop into the water to clean the sand from her body, the result of dramatic volleyball saves. She's been doing this all week; it's a no brainer.

Unbeknownst to her, moments earlier at the next resort, lifeguards have seen two large sharks cruising the shallow ocean. This is extremely unusual and they hastily alert their guests to get out of the water, but they never pass the warning down the beach.

Nicole ventures out waist deep, as she has already done many times that week. She's alone, most guests having headed back up the patio for pre-lunch drinks. She smiles to herself, looking forward to the scuba adventure she is about to enjoy.

Nicole isn't swimming, just walking around in the shallows, the water being no higher than her waist. She uses her hands to splash off the offending grit. She doesn't know it but this simple action is creating a disturbance in the sea.

She looks up and catches a glimpse of two Jet Ski drivers waving at her. They are yelling in Spanish. She waves back and laughs. Nicole doesn't speak Spanish. At first she assumes they are just having fun. "Crazy guys."

What she doesn't know is that they are telling her to get out of the water. They've seen the two sharks and are trying to warn her while attempting to scare *los tiburones* back into the deep.

One shark leaves. But the other is persistent.

The guys use their Jet Skis to try to agitate the menacing animal. They've been at it for several minutes, trying to herd the shark like cattle.

Then, in a decision that is questionable at best, they try ramming it, annoying the unyielding creature, encouraging the bull shark's innate aggressive nature. But this vicious predator does not scare easily. Instead of turning out to the boundless ocean, it veers inward, ready to fight back.

The Jet Ski guys yell once again to Nicole. Only now does she realize they are not out for fun. Something is wrong.

She pivots quickly, looking toward the beach. So near yet so far.

She begins to wade in, but the bull shark is just feet away. Possibly mistaking Nicole for a fish in dire straits, or the perpetrator of those hostile attacks from above, it approaches with amazing velocity. Instinctively doing what its ancestors have done for centuries: accelerating to investigate. The animal bumps her to establish what's there.

Nicole turns. What the hell was that?

Her heart sinks. She realizes what has happened.

Panic sets in, and before she can blink the first strike comes with lightning speed from the murkiness below.

The shark rips into her upper left thigh. Its barbed, knife-like teeth tear apart her flesh and muscles.

The impact is massive.

The shark yanks away more than a foot of skin and everything underneath from Nicole's leg.

She will later learn that two quadriceps and two hamstrings have been ripped from her leg in less time than it takes to state that fact.

The gaping wound goes right to the femur, the strongest bone of the human skeleton.

This incredible action is later described by a doctor as "incredibly clean, amazingly concise: just as straight a cut as if it were done by a surgeon taking his time with a finely honed scalpel."

The ocean is instantly ablaze with bright, billowing red blood.

Nicole feels no pain. She later remarks, "Some surfer dude from California said, 'If you can imagine how bad a shark bite is, it's worse.' I disagree. At the time — maybe because of shock and trauma — I didn't sense pain at all. I just knew how much trouble I was in. I knew this could very well be the end."

She also knows that sharks like blood. And she is surrounded by it. She needs to get out of there. But moving isn't going to happen quickly. The shark has already destroyed her left quadraplex and hamstring muscles. Her leg is next to useless.

She has to focus solely on surviving — every effort must be made to save her own life.

But the ferocious bull shark is not done with her. In a flash, it circles around her body and lunges at her left arm, clenching the limb in its rapacious jaws, squeezing with monumental pressure.

Nicole can't believe what is happening. "No!" she screams.

The monster has her entire arm locked in its mouth. It is biting hard, and is about to pull her down into the depths.

Is this the way my children will lose their mother? flashes through her mind.

She catches a momentary glimpse of her attacker's horrifying, lifeless black eyes. It's an image she'll never forget. So penetrating, yet so indifferent.

The force of the shark is unbelievable, but somehow, summoning inhuman strength from some primordial instinct, Nicole raises her right fist and smashes it down on the animal's nose. Just like that, the idea springing to her mind from out of nowhere. Determined to fight fire with fire.

At the same time she yanks her left arm toward her body. To her great surprise and relief, she actually manages to loosen the predator's grip.

The bull shark lets go, convinced that she is not a meal worth savouring nor a foe worth menacing further. It dives down deeper and swims off.

Nicole is left flailing in the sea of blood. Experiencing a lethal mix of shock and trauma, she is in danger of losing consciousness. But she knows the bull shark is known for letting its prey bleed to death and then returning to finish the meal minutes later.

Will it be back?

So much has happened so quickly, it is impossible to compute what anything means. Time slows down for Nicole.

Her left arm is hanging, barely there. Her left leg won't move. And the sea continues quickly turning crimson, full of her blood, which is pouring from her body with alarming speed.

Her attempts at movement against the weight of the water are sluggish, lacking in energy.

She looks out to the Jet Ski drivers through blurry eyes. She struggles to maintain self-control and a sound mind.

Summoning up her fading staying power, she breathlessly calls out, "You need ... to get me ... out of here!" She fears her exhausted strength and dimming stamina will not be enough to even push the words forward.

They sit on their machines, immobile.

She wonders if they have heard her.

They seemed stunned by what has occurred.

Suddenly one of them seems to realize his actions could make the difference between losing a life and saving one.

After checking to ensure the shark is gone, he accelerates and advances toward Nicole's flailing body, now badly in danger of slipping beneath the waves. He grabs her hand as best he could and begins towing her to shore.

Passersby will later recall that a thirty-foot trail of blood covered the surface of the sea behind her, she was bleeding so badly. The shark's sharp serrated teeth have done just what they were meant to do: rip her apart.

The Jet Ski guy has no experience with this. Fighting shock himself, he struggles to stay alert and work his way to shore. He beaches the machine, jumps off, and yanks Nicole, face down, onto the sand in a clumsy yet life-saving move.

He stands back, unsure.

He will later confess that he was unable to actually look at her battered, bloody body. He figured she was *moribundo* — next to dead. Beyond help.

A crowd begins to form. Spanish and English voices echo in Nicole's ears as she lies on the sand.

Breathing is strenuous. Gruelling. Her lungs feel like unyielding gym weights.

Finally someone realizes they need to turn her over. They pull her body around so she is face up. She's covered in blood, sand, and seawater.

She feels like she is burning up under the blistering noon Mexican sun, which scalds her eyes.

The people around her are in shock — dazed. They move in plodding slow motion, unsure, insensitive to her needs.

She tries to muster what little of her ebbing strength she can. Somehow she has to find the will to take a medical inventory.

She can only imagine what she will find.

As onlookers gape in shock, Nicole pushes at the sagging sand. At first she is unsuccessful. But she is strong, if only momentarily. She raises her head and shoulders ever so slightly and manages to glimpse down at her leg. At her arm.

Only then does she realize just how severe her wounds are, how desperate her situation is.

And only then does she accept that her chances of escaping this incident alive are next to nil.

"Help me ..." she gaspes as her head falls back to the sand.

Nicole's voice jolts the people around her. They seem to awake from their stupor.

Amazingly, her arm is intact, although a huge chunk has been ripped from it. Bystanders see the massive hole in her leg, exposed to the bone. Many turn away, unable to stomach such horror. It is not a sight for the faint of heart.

Nicole is so traumatized, so exhausted. All she wants to do is sleep.

But that would be a deep sleep she may not wake from. Her medical training tells her that giving in to slumber is akin to saying a final *adiós*.

"Talk ... to ... me!" she gasps to anyone who will listen. "Keep me awake ... please! Talk to ... me ..." she appeals in a fading voice.

She has lost so much blood that breathing is nearly impossible. A coursing stream of blood squirts from her leg, jetting more than a foot in the air, every time her heart beats.

A bystander finally registers that unless they stop the flow of blood immediately this woman is going to die. He rushes forward, pushes himself into the thick of the action, and reaches around her leg. He applies pressure to the artery with his big hands, restricting the spewing blood, at least temporarily.

"Talk ... to ... me ..." she gasps again. "Keep me awake ... please ... talk ... to ... me ..." she appeals in a fading voice.

But the last thing she really wants to do is remain awake, aware. It is a struggle. Her body is spent, waning, ready to shut down.

"Don't ... let ... me ... go ... to ... sleep ..."

She is barely able to get the words out now.

Fighting to keep aware of her surroundings, she wonders why she is still bleeding.

She realizes no one has attended to her arm wounds.

She can see the slight pulsing of an arterial bleed.

"Tourniquet … my … arm…." she gasps.

People try to do what they can for her. But they are worried. The pasty colour of Nicole's face indicates that death is near.

She has lost over 60 percent of her blood. It's rare for anyone to survive that.

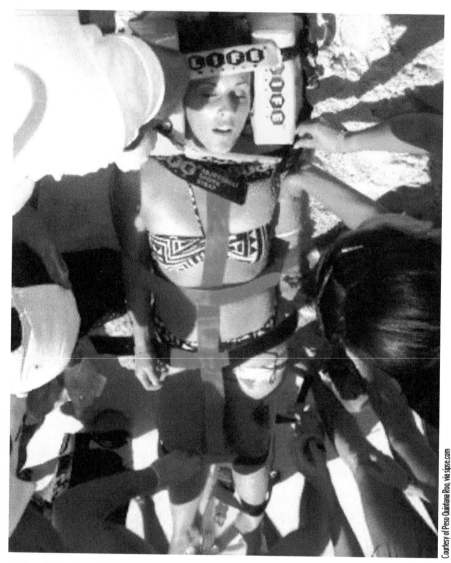

Nicole on the backboard on the beach.

A bystander whispers, "She's going to die. You don't lose that amount of blood and survive. You just don't."

"Keep me ... don't ... don't ... please ..." she sputters with failing stamina.

Breathing has become almost impossible. Nicole is suffocating.

"Get a backboard to put her on!" someone screams.

A siren blares amidst the shouting. An ambulance.

Nicole's eyes glaze over. She can no longer focus. As strong as she is — as resilient — she is losing her battle for life. Her heart is running out of strength to pump.

There is now barely any pulse at all.

She knows with certainty that she may die at any moment.

There seems to be little anyone can do other than look on in dismay and terror. Others turn away, unable to bear witness to what will surely be a life's end.

In fact, if you were there on the beach that awful day in January, you'd have been forgiven for bursting into tears watching the sad scene of this vibrant, dynamic lady about to fade from existence.

Suddenly, paramedics, screaming in Spanish, appear on the beach. They know they need to get Nicole onto that backboard and to a hospital in seconds.

They get to work, strapping her body down on the board. Then they begin their harsh journey.

They trudge through the hot, heavy sand.

It's like trekking through the Sahara at high noon: merciless.

Finally reaching the hotel, they veer through the public areas to where the ambulance sits waiting. The Grand Park's fancy guests gasp into their margaritas. "What the hell?"

The young ambulance driver is clearly rattled. He has never experienced anything like this before.

But what he does know is how to drive quickly. Maybe a little too quickly. As he puts the pedal to the metal, Nicole's stretcher, which has not been secured well, bounces around as they mount bumps and careen around curves.

Meanwhile, the paramedics are struggling to get IV access. In fact, they strive to get any blood-pressure reading at all.

But they made it to Hospiten Cancún, which is the first hospital in Quintana Roo to obtain the Consejo de Salubridad General certificate, endorsing it as a healthcare institution providing the best level of care. (It's a claim that will be seriously questioned months later.)

By the time Nicole is taken to the trauma room, she is no longer able to breathe.

The ER team quickly assess the situation. They have no time to waste. This is clearly a crisis — one that could go either way.

6

From All Angles

To fully appreciate what has happened we need to hear from a number of voices on the beach.

First is Nicole. Listening to her tell the story is chilling. But as you consider her account, ask yourself: could you have handled this without the medical training she was so fortunate to be able to fall back on?

Nicole Moore:

There was no foreboding that day, no sense that something might go wrong. Some people get those feelings, I know, but I had no omen that something unique — something truly awful — was in store for me.

The shark bumping me from behind: it was just like a toddler walking into you at the grocery store. No biggie. But then, in a millisecond: panic, an instant sinking feeling in my stomach.

And then the bite. The first bite.

People asked me later if I screamed. I didn't. I guess there was just no time. I'm also asked about pain. But I just don't recall feeling pain. In a Discovery Channel Shark Week episode I heard Australian Navy diver Paul de Gelder describe his encounter with a bull shark as, "It hurt like I can't possibly describe … I pretty much thought I was dead." But for me, I just didn't experience anything like that. I can't recall feeling any pain at all.

However, after the shark has bumped me, what I do know instantly is that it's taken a big bite out of my left upper thigh ... this shark's gone through my leg just like it was eating butter.

I also know I've got to get out of the water.

I start using my arms to help propel me to shore. I have no idea what kind of damage has happened to my leg at this point, but I've got no strength in that limb: it's just a dead weight.

And I'm surrounded by a sea of blood, amazingly quick.

I struggle to move forward in the water. I'm trying my best, but without muscles in my left leg to thrust me onward, it's so slow.

I sense I'm not going to get to the beach on time.

And then my arm. The shark suddenly swims back and yanks my entire arm into its mouth! I can't believe it!

Those eyes: dull, expressionless, incredibly scary eyes, yet so full of fury at the same time. It's hard to describe.

We are looking eye to eye ... really black, void eyes, creepy eyes, creepy things to look at.

I just remember this massive head looking straight back at me ... its gums pulled back with its teeth showing.

I'm thrashing in the water and I realize the shark is trying to pull me down. I'm trying desperately to do something, anything ...

To this day, I don't know where the resilience came to smash this huge shark with my right fist. I mean, I guess it could have gone either way: annoy him so he leaves, or anger him more so he intensifies the attack. But it worked! He swims away.

I'm panicked. I need to get to shore before this thing comes back. Is it going to finish me off? It's the ultimate feeling of terror: is it going to come and get me again? The panic of what's beneath the water.

I don't know why the Jet Ski guys aren't moving in, aren't coming close enough. They must be as frightened as I am.

But after I scream out, one of them finally circles around and comes in closer. I jump with everything I have in my right leg and we reach out and lock fingertips, literally just fingertips. He guns it to shore and beaches the Jet Ski, pulling me along with him. That's how I end up face down in the sand, I guess.

Eventually someone grabs me and flips me over. The bright sunlight is blinding.

My clear recollection of events at this point is perhaps a little faded now, but I know I'm lying in the sand, trying to figure out how badly I'm hurt. I recall seeing my arm kind of lacerated there.

I know this is not good.

But the funny thing is, everyone seems transfixed, shocked, and no one is doing anything. I remember gasping, "Help me … you have to help me…."

The next thing is this huge pair of hands just slamming down on my leg. Apparently the blood flow was really excessive, and this amazing man gives no thought to possible contamination to himself, or his personal safety or the risks of exposure to germs or infections, he just puts his hands on my leg wound and stops the spurting streams of blood. I get this warm feeling that someone's doing something. Don't recall his face … don't recall anyone's face …

I look up and see a pretty girl telling me she's a nurse. Is she an angel? Wait, no, there are two nurses. They just happened to be near the beach. They're trying to help. I turn to one of them, and at this point I'm barely gasping: "Keep talking to me. You need to keep me awake."

I keep struggling to stay awake … struggling to breathe. I just want it to be all over so I can go to sleep. I'm so tired … so hot … so …

But as much as I know I need to stay with it, I feel a warm sensation around me. I look at my arm and there is this huge puddle of blood. "My arm … my arm," I say to anyone who will listen, "I need a tourniquet."

Without missing a beat, some guy just whips the tie string out of his shorts and one of the nurses creates a tourniquet.

I just want to go to sleep.

I'm drifting into respiratory distress.

I'm trying to think logically, trying to handle this information overload like a nurse. I know I'm hypovolemic, the shock that accompanies low blood volume. I know that if I don't have enough blood in my system, my heart can't pump enough to my lungs. And if blood doesn't get to my lungs, the oxygen exchange won't happen, which will cause respiratory distress.

So I know that, lying on the beach with a chewed up arm and leg, both bleeding profusely in the heat of the noonday sun, I'm in a really, really bad way.

Think, Nicole, think!

If I don't get the help I need soon, the next stage is that my heart won't be able to pump adequately. I'll go into V-fib: ventricular fibrillation, where your heart just flutters and eventually stops. And then you die.

So as I'm lying there, panicked, lethargic, covered in sand and blood, hot ... I know I need to slow my breathing down. I need to slow my heart rate down.

I convince myself to keep breathing as much as I can, but as slow as I can.

I need to keep calm, to keep my heart rate down. It's an absolute conscious decision on my part that I need to do this and fight for every last minute.

But keeping calm in the wake of what's happened ... well ... not easily done, to say the least!

Okay, just for a minute, let me see if I can give you a sense of what this was like. Put your hand over your nose and mouth. Just let only a bit of air through. Or put a pillow over your face. Then force your breathing to slow down. Your heart will go through this little flutter as your brain wants you to breathe more. But you can't. Your brain is trying to talk sense to you, but everything you're doing is not helping the situation.

Well, that's just what it was like.

So, I'm lying there. I know how easy it is to panic. But I've got to focus on trying to keep calm.

Time seems like an eternity, but by now I'm truly anxious. I'm trying to simplify everything, but I can't get rid of thoughts about my kids. I'm going to die, I'll never see my kids, my husband, my father, again....

Wait! That's just not an option! I've got to keep breathing no matter what it takes, but slowly, no panic, slow breaths ... focus on the shallow breaths, focus on staying awake.

But then everything shifts. Hardly able to breathe any more ... trying to tell myself to stay awake ... tell people they need to keep me awake ... they need to keep talking to me ... but I just can't stay awake anymore.

And suddenly there is this overwhelming pure bright light. Enveloping. Calming. So peaceful. It's an embrace ... so comforting ... bright white. It's giving me a sense of ... I don't know ... serenity.

Is it the doorway between earth and heaven? Is it the chemical response to stress? Blood loss? Endorphins? I don't know.

Tranquility ... it's really nice ... soooo pleasing ... so welcoming.

And I'm certain of one thing. Without a doubt, I'm at death's door.

What I am experiencing is what people feel when they die. I used to see it in my patients when they'd go through this calm, peaceful period. I'm getting ready to die, here, on the beach, covered in sand and sweat and blood.

But somehow, by whatever intervention, I'm allowed to stay and fight.

I shake my head, re-grip my sanity, push away the urge to surrender. I can't go there, I'm thinking, I can't go to sleep. Not today. I have to fight for my life, my kids, my family. Have to keep me awake. Have to keep my eyes open.

Focus, Nicole!

Where the hell is everybody? Why aren't they moving me away from here? What's going on?

Finally a backboard arrives. They shift me onto it.

The pain of that movement is dreadful.

They tie me down.

Someone's yelling questions at me, going for the person/place/time orientation. But I can't breathe. And I'm so hot — the noonday sun is beating down on me and it feels like a thousand degrees.

And then they are carrying me ... they're going through really tough sand on a beach that's not meant for swift travelling. And the whole backboard is tossing and turning and bumping...

They're so exhausted, these guys carrying me. They have to stop and catch their breath. But all I'm thinking is, "I don't know how much longer I can hold on, please keep going!"

It's a huge beach. It's taking them ... well, it seems like hours.

And then they have to carry me through the resort, onto the patio, through the lobby, to a side door. People are standing there starring, shocked, disbelieving. One moment they're lounging by the pool with their margaritas and the next ... well, you can imagine.

But at last I'm in the shade. At least that coolness feels better.

And then the ambulance. The poor young driver has never seen anything like this before. He's experiencing sheer terror ... he just doesn't know what to make of it. So he does what he thinks makes sense: hits the accelerator to the floor!

But they haven't been able to secure me very well in this bumpy, potholed, careening ambulance. I'm bouncing all over the place in a race against time.

Now, I've never even told my family what I'm about to say ...

At this point, my body has started to shut down peripherally. My skin has turned cold and clammy. I can't feel my extremities or my face. The end is very near: this is as grave as it gets. The circulation has slowed to my legs and arms and hands ... my brain is just sending everything I have left to my vital organs. But they're shutting down. It's bad.

And then, my bowels just let go ... I feel so bad for the driver. "I'm so sorry..." I'm gasping, always the one who wants to make everything nice for everybody else. The poor soul ...

My training tells me what this means: I've got mere minutes now left on my lifespan. It's just my heart and my brain that are remaining and they're down for the count. Once my heart checks out, I've got two minutes before brain damage.

Clearly, Nicole's depth of medical training helped her stay alive, but also informed her that she was likely about to die.

So, what's worse: knowing or not knowing?

While you ponder that, let's hear from Roy Clark of Moundsville, West Virginia. He was enjoying a relaxed Cancún vacation with his wife, Sharon. This is a man with absolutely no medical training at all, who never stopped to ask questions or worry about his own safety. He just stepped in and acted intuitively to help save Nicole Moore's life.

Roy Clark

We'd set out to spend the day walking the beach when we noticed lifeguards demanding people get out of the water. Then two men got on Jet Skis and it appeared they were trying to chase something away from the beach. It reminded me of a western with cowboys on horses herding cattle; instead, it was Mexicans on Jet Skis trying to direct sharks back out into the ocean.

We watched for a bit, but kept walking north up the beach toward the Grand Park Royal. We didn't get far — maybe fifty to seventy-five yards. Suddenly I saw someone in trouble in the water. At that point, all I could see was her head. I didn't know if she was standing or floating … then a Jet Ski pulled beside her and the driver grabbed hold and dragged her to shore. From fifty yards away I could see a blood trail in the water. It was easily thirty-feet long. Unbelievable!

"We need to hurry," I said to Sharon. "That girl is bleeding so badly."

As I approached, they'd rolled her onto her back, where she was lying on the sand. There was a Mexican fellow standing there. He didn't seem to know what to do. I immediately tried to assess the damage. Blood was squirting from her left leg, had to be easily twelve to fourteen inches in the air every time her heart beat. I dropped to my knees and quickly began applying pressure with my hands on the artery. It worked: the flow of blood began to slow down.

The girl looked up and asked if I spoke English. "I do. But tell me your name and where you're staying." I was trying to figure out her level of consciousness. She passed the test.

It was only then I saw the destruction was not confined to her leg. Her left arm had severe damage on the inside. It was bleeding with body fluids mixing with blood.

Someone suddenly appeared with a quarter-inch piece of rope: he wanted to put a tourniquet on Nicole's leg. But I had the blood stopped and wouldn't let him use it. I think he saw how badly she'd been bleeding and holding pressure on the artery had stopped it — he respected that and backed off.

At one point, a nurse came in — I'm guessing three to five minutes after I got there. She was good at keeping Nicole awake, not letting her fall into a sleep. As for me, I pretty much had everything else around me tuned out. I know there were a lot of people standing around, but my focus was solely on keeping that left leg from bleeding. I lost all recollection of what was taking place while I was applying pressure on that artery, right up until we placed her on the backboard. My surroundings were totally tuned out.

Soon, medical people arrived. An EMT wrapped some kind of bandage around her leg above the wound. It was an elastic wrap one-and-a-half to two-inches wide, and, frankly, I didn't think it would work. But I knew I had to let go, so I released the pressure. I watched to make sure it wasn't going to start pumping blood again. Sure enough, it looked like the wrap would do its job.

Someone had retrieved a backboard and I helped put Nicole on it. I heard the siren from the ambulance. Then it hit me: Nicole's condition was much worse than critical. I saw firsthand how severe the wounds to her leg and arm were. The amount of blood she lost was unbelievable. I saw that glazed over look in her eyes ... that stare ...

After they took her to the ambulance, I remember turning to

Sharon and saying, "Nicole is going to die." I just didn't see how anyone could survive that. You just can't lose that amount of blood and experience that amount of shock and trauma and live. Even if everyone who helped Nicole that day had done everything perfectly, I didn't think it would be enough.

But somehow she survived. I have no doubt at all that it's a miracle. It's a miracle.

Days later, Roy and his wife visited Nicole in the ICU. They held her hands and offered a prayer. "It was moving, really moving," Nicole recalls. "Such heartfelt words from total strangers."

Carlos Da Silva is the general manager of the Grand Park Royal Cancún Caribe hotel. This experienced, elegant man reacted with professionalism, treading cautiously into untested waters, having no previous experience with a shark attack.

Carlos Da Silva

CODE BLUE! It's enough to alert my attention at any time of the day or night that's there's something seriously wrong. And that's what I heard on January 31, 2011, just as I was preparing to go to lunch. Code Blue is our danger signal for anything that might happen at the beach. We'd never had a shark incident before so we don't have a code for that. Still, I immediately knew there was some kind of problem. I've been in the hotel management business for thirty-five years, here and overseas. I've had people die from various causes … I've experienced a hotel fire … you know, things happen. But this was my first experience with a shark. And frankly, none of us were prepared for that.

I ran down to the beach and found a lot of people gathered there. And then I saw this girl lying on the sand. My God, it was awful … she was so pale. My first reaction was to give her space. There were so many people all over the place … taking pictures…. I yelled out "Clear the area!" and got people to move back.

Once we thought we had the situation under control, I called up to our office and said, "I need an ambulance here now!" The receptionist asked why and I said, "Don't ask! Just get it here!"

We waited ... it was probably only a couple minutes but it felt like hours. I knew this was life or death and we couldn't delay. I called back up to the office. The girl told me, "Carlos, I called the ambulance! They're on their way!"

"We can't wait!" I told her. "Call another one!"

We ended up with two ambulances coming, but that's okay. The first one got Nicole to the hospital in record time.

It was shocking. I've never experienced anything like this. I mean, even all the records here in Cancún show that to see a shark that close to the beach is a one in a million chance. It just doesn't happen.

Clasien Carlsen was sunning with her friend Brittney Leigh, up by the hotel's infinity pool. They'd discussed going swimming in the ocean — something the two twenty-five-year-old nurses from Portland, Oregon, had done each day on their vacation so far ... at the *exact spot* where Nicole was attacked. But Brittney begged off on this Monday.

"Let's just hang out by the pool today, Clasien," she'd offered to her friend. "I don't feel much like going to the beach."

Her decision may well have saved her life.

Clasien Carlsen

We were just sitting there when we noticed a whole bunch of guests running to the beach. We couldn't really see what was going on because there was a huge mass of people right at the water's edge. I was thinking it was maybe a near-drowning. I was wondering if we should go? I mean, as a nurse, you're supposed to help ... but I'm a neonatal intensive care nurse handling babies at Providence Portland Medical Center: what skill do I have to offer? Anyway, we decided we had to go: we're nurses.

There had to be at least thirty people there, with more arriving. At first, they were preventing us from getting near. Brittney and I are running up but they were saying in Spanish, "No! No! Get away! Get away!" They wanted to keep everyone back from her so they could try to attend to her. But we kept saying, "We're nurses, we can help!" We're trying to communicate with them between our English and their Spanish, which wasn't easy. But once they understood, they pretty much just shoved us right up to Nicole.

As soon as I saw her, I said, "Oooohhh crap!" It was horrific. We were not expecting that at all. It was shocking. I mean, you could see this huge chunk missing out of her leg and her arm … man, it was just shredded. She was so pale … you could tell she needed oxygen.

And you could also tell right away just by looking at it: shark attack. There was no doubt.

And then I thought: We have zero training for this!

As soon as we got over that quick shock, both Brittney and I … our nursing experience just clicked in right away. It was just jump in and apply pressure on her arm to try to stabilize things. Mind you, before we got there, someone had done a pretty good job of applying tourniquets to her shredded arm to minimize the blood flow and stabilize it.

She was pretty relieved we spoke English and she was surprisingly alert. She really wanted us to keep her awake. But she'd fade in and out.

"Just keep talking to me, keep asking me questions" … that's how we learned she was a nurse from Canada. Everyone was trying to help us, like bringing out the little stretcher and trying to get oxygen. We wanted to start an IV but there was nothing to make that work. We knew we needed to get fluids into her.

Things were happening so quickly. No one person was in charge. Except Nicole, really. Someone — a lifeguard or somebody — tried to put an oxygen mask with a reservoir bag over her face to help her breathe, but we kept shoving him out of the way because she's talking and she's breathing … she's blue, okay, but she doesn't need anyone to breathe for her at that point. I kept saying, "Get away from her! You're not helping the situation!" Of course, they didn't speak English … but I finally made myself understood and he backed off. You feel bad because everyone wants to help, but that wasn't going to be any help at all.

We stayed with her until the ambulance came. Throughout, she was amazingly strong. She was calm, she wasn't ballistic, she wasn't crazy. She was with it, and even talking us through with some stuff to do. She was remarkable, we couldn't believe it.

Nick Smith, from Mankato, Minnesota, just happened to be walking down the beach with a couple of his buddies.

Nick Smith

We're just strolling along when suddenly we hear people yelling. We look back and just see red in the water about a hundred yards away. We know that isn't good. We instantly rush to see if we can help. We're right there when they pull her up on the beach. From there, it's all a blur how fast things were happening. There was a nurse asking about tying a tourniquet on Nicole's leg. She looked at us and yelled for another string. My friend was able to quickly rip the string off his shorts and hand it to the girl so she could tie it around Nicole's arm. After that we were screaming for people to hurry with the stretcher. But we just felt so helpless. Everything just felt so surreal.

Carlos Da Silva

What is truly amazing is that Nicole was awake for some of this time. She was actually directing us what to do and what not to do. I don't know how she did that ... her nursing training was what made the difference, I think. If she didn't have that experience, I can assure you it would have been very difficult for us to deal with everything.

Donna Holwell

Some of us had headed into town to do some shopping, but Nicole being Nicole wanted to stay to play volleyball. I remember getting back and all of us wanted a cold beer and a swim. But suddenly people were approaching us saying, "Shark attack." It was surreal: you felt like you weren't in that moment. Awful. It really felt like you were in a horror movie, like *Jaws* or something. You think to yourself: is this really happening to us? Part of you just doesn't want to believe it. And at this point, no one had even said anything about it being Nicole who was attacked.

Terri Holden

I remember, I think it was Toni ... she told us, "You won't believe this but apparently a shark attack has occurred. It happened to a young lady." We looked at each other with a sigh of relief: thank goodness it's not us because we're not young! Of course I was forgetting that Nicole was younger than us and looked even younger. One of the girls who played volleyball with us came up and said, "Terri, you heard about the shark attack?"

I said, "Yeah, we're just hearing about it now."

She had a funny look on her face. She seemed awkward. Then she said, "I think it might have been Nicole."

My heart stopped.

I still get emotional ... she was on that trip because she came for me. I've had that in the back of my mind, unfortunately. I feel somewhat responsible that she was there. And I know she wouldn't want me to feel that way, but I can't help it.

Anyway, my reaction was sheer terror. I could feel my heart start to race. The girl said to me, "Those two ladies over there are nurses and they helped." I turned to see who she was pointing to and saw Nicole's beach bag sitting on the chair. I knew immediately that it was her. We went and spoke to the nurses but I can't recall a thing they said. All I could focus on was getting to the hospital. I felt very panicked.

Carlos Da Silva

After the ambulance left, William, my head of security, and I were standing there trying to make sense of it. But all of a sudden, I noticed something floating in the water. "What is that?" I asked.

"Oh my God," he said, "it's the part that the shark ripped off her leg!"

It was almost her whole thigh. While he grabbed it, I called up for a plastic bag full of ice so we could try to preserve it and get it to the hospital. I was told they tried to reattach that piece during the eight hours they operated.

Cyndi Cramer

I just remember coming back from shopping and hearing some mumbling about a young woman being attacked by a shark. I'm not one to intrude on anyone's conversation, but this one lady was a little bit louder than the others, quite distraught. I turned around and she said, "A young woman," and I thought, "Oh good, that's not our group. We're fifty plus, so we're all good. And that was the end of it as far as I was concerned. And it's funny, the way she was saying it, it didn't sound like it was life threatening in any way…

But then Terri came up toward us. Just the look on her face: I kind of looked at her and thought, "Oh my God." I didn't even think shark attack, I just thought something was seriously wrong. But she came to our table and told us about it, about it being Nicole. My reaction was just … just sort of disbelief. Then I'm thinking, okay, there was a little bite, that's all. Nothing compared to what it turned out to be.

But Terri had talked to the nurses and learned about a big chunk being taken out of Nicole's leg … it didn't even register about the arm after that. It was just, "Oh my God…" and I didn't really grasp the severity of it until we were all sitting there later in the hospital and it was taking so long, and I guess I finally realized: this is a life-and-death situation.

Ken Mihan

I'd driven the ladies into town to shop, and after we got back to the hotel I went looking for Nicole, because we were going scuba diving that afternoon. I saw the Jet Skis flying around and then suddenly a mass of red in the ocean. You know what I said? "Those idiots have hit someone with the Jet Ski!"

But next I saw them dragging a body up on the shore and I ran down there. And it was Nicole! I was shocked! I couldn't believe it. Like, every day, I'd been right there. This one day, I agree to take the ladies shopping and this happens. It might have been me. But how could this be happening to poor Nicole?

Those two nurses and that guy Roy were on her in a heartbeat. The nurses just happened to be near the beach. Everybody was yelling for a board, yelling for oxygen…. Nicole was fighting for her life, but managed to tell them to put the tourniquet on. How the hell she was in the right mind to tell them what needed to be done I'll never know.

Clasien Carlsen

I think Brittney and I made a significant amount of difference that day. We were able to provide our own set of nursing care to her body, and I think just the emotional aspect of our being there really helped relieve her and gave her the courage to hold on … it's even soothing to be able to communicate with someone like us, because Nicole didn't speak Spanish. It definitely would have been worse without us there, I think.

Terri Holden

We found out that Janet was on the way to the hospital with Nicole's thigh in a box beside her. Poor Janet! Donna and I ran to the front of the hotel to grab a cab to the hospital when we learned the hotel manager had already taken Ken and Janet there.

It was a long drive: so many things race through your mind and all I could think of was, "Please let her survive." Just the terror in that girl's eyes when she said she thought it was Nicole … I knew something bad had happened. It's a very surreal experience to go through something so traumatic. I remembered the feeling when they told me my husband had died. I remember being taken into the room to identify his body… it's what comes flooding back to you when you go through a traumatic experience like this.

Kathy Sutton

There are no other words for it: I was just shocked, stunned. I was in a state of disbelief.

Sandra Schad

I agree: total shock. And you know, when we first heard about the injuries I thought they'll just stitch her back up and she'll be fine. It's just a little bite: just clean it up and stitch it up. But then we learned she'd had this huge surgery and she was in critical condition …

I was shocked.

7

Struggle for Survival: Mexico

Imagine the fear — the stark terror — of opening your eyes, blinking, and then realizing you have absolutely no capacity to comprehend anything at all. *Where the hell are you?*

Suddenly you see lifeless eyes, a sickening fish-form lunging at your leg and then your arm, razor-like teeth sinking into your flesh. Only then do you start to understand you're not flailing helplessly in the ocean, you are not lying near death on the sand. But if you're not at the beach fighting off a shark, where are you? *Where are your friends? What's happened to your kids?*

The fog begins to lift. The penny drops. You're lying in a bed in some kind of weird room. It's not your room. It's not a hotel room. *Where are you? What's going on? What are those noises?*

You blink again and raise your head slightly to take stock. Then it hits you. The pain! The excruciating pain that jolts through your body. You try to scream, unable to deal with the intense soreness. It's like nothing you've ever confronted before. Childbirth was a walk in the park compared to what's currently racking your body.

You close your eyes, trying desperately to shut it all out. But somewhere in the back of your mind a little voice tells you to stay awake, to keep fighting, to survive.

So it was on that awful winter day in 2011 that this was Nicole Moore's reality as she regained consciousness, lying in a hospital bed in Mexico.

"I have so many memories of that time," she says. "I was trying to take a deep breath to centre myself, but I found I couldn't. In fact, I couldn't catch my breath at all. Then I realized there was a tube down my throat. And then I noticed a ventilator. *What the...?*

"After the attack, I had been fighting so desperately to cling to life, accepting that this was surely the most difficult struggle I'd ever endured. And it seemed to go on forever.

"I even remember in the trauma room ... the scissors ... there's this nurse brandishing them, coming at me. *What?* Then I realize she's ready to cut off the expensive bathing suit my dad had bought for me as a vacation present. Desperately I try to tell her that there is a clasp ... she doesn't need to cut ... but it's futile. *Snip.* It's gone.

"How odd that I'm dying but I'm worried about a meaningless thing like a bathing suit."

While Nicole didn't know it at the time, the ER team was racing against the clock to keep her alive. Saving a bathing suit took second place to saving a life.

"I recall a doctor saying they need to insert a central line directly into my heart. And I notice they have difficulty inserting it. 'Have they punctured my lung during this procedure?' I ask myself. 'Wait a minute ... it's starting to add up. But what then? *Come on Nic* ... you're a nurse ... you can do this ... you can figure this out.'"

Dr. Rafael Velasco supervised the eight-hour operation, during which the medical team pumped in unit upon unit of blood and blood product to keep Nicole's heart working. Later on what would surprise her and her family was that this complex operation was summed up in a sparse two-paragraph report. They would be horrified to learn it was merely a cursory account with no detail at all, not even in chronological order.

"I was so groggy and in a state of stressful upheaval," Nicole recalls. "Awakening from the procedure brought total panic for me. I was truly unsure if I was even alive. Had I lost my arm? My leg? Did I go into cardiac arrest? Had I died? I knew nothing and there seemed to be no one around to give me answers. The sense of isolation and uncertainty was overwhelming. What had just happened to me? What had I lived through? Or *had* I lived through it? What kind of trauma was I experiencing? What was the outcome?

"It was *awful*. I woke up alone and disoriented. I'm on a breathing machine. There's a tube down my throat and no one can help me understand why. What was going on? Where was I? I was scared, and I don't scare easily. And the pain … so much pain. It was truly terrible."

The medical team had left her on a ventilator for full life support. The machine was set to breathe for Nicole at a rate determined by the doctor. But her waking brain wanted to take over and breathe at her own pace. The ventilator was unyielding, however, not allowing for the heightened demand. Nicole's heart rate increased.

Alarms were going off.

"I started to panic … the worst feeling ever."

But it was about to become worse.

Nicole began feeling like she had a pillow over her head. Her sensation was of being slowly suffocated. With no one around, she'd have to figure this one out alone. *Think, Nicole! What does your nursing training tell you?* She fell back on a memory, having worked with these machines before. She realized her only choice was to try to work *with* it, to try to breathe along *with* this device, rather than struggle. *Don't fight the flow,* she told herself.

Breathe in … pause. Breathe out … pause. Breathe in … pause …

Finally, Dr. Jesús Álvarez Tostado Romero-Valdéz strode into the room. As best she could, Nicole scrawled out a note asking him to take the tube out. But he paid no attention to her. He smiled, even laughed, telling her in a patronizing manner that they had some concerns: "We don't think you can breathe on your own right now." But Nicole was shaking her head, trying to tell him she did not require this breathing machine. She knew she could breathe without it. "No, no, it's okay. Trust me, you need this," the doctor kept saying.

The reading the doctor saw — an abnormal ECG (the test that interprets electrical activity of the heart) — made him fear that if he put any further strain on Nicole it might cause other problems, or even cardiac arrest. "We have some cardiac concerns," he kept telling her. What he did not know was that Nicole's abnormal ECG is, in fact, normal for her. She'd had it for years. Relentlessly, she kept insisting they remove the tube. Finally he extubated her, only to find she was, in fact, breathing fine on her own without the vent. It was truly a relief to the poor nurse from Canada, whose knowledge of her own system outweighed the doctor's.

"Next, I remember learning that a shark had ripped a large flap of skin and muscle tissue from my thigh, but that it had been found and brought to the hospital by my friends. Apparently the doctors had reattached it to my leg."

Later Nicole would learn that this procedure had been completed without any attempt to add a blood supply, meaning there was only one result that could occur: the flap would rot. Nicole also discovered that her arm was badly torn, but apparently the medics felt it could be saved. Still, it seemed as though they'd done nothing other than bandage it.

On the second day in the hospital, Nicole realized her hand was turning black. No one was doing anything about it.

On the third day, she could hardly move her arm at all. She insisted someone investigate.

"All they told me was, 'The circulation's not there. We've tried to improve the blood flow. We've done all we can for you.'"

Not very reassuring, to say the least.

What Nicole was also unaware of is that hours before the initiation of any procedures, Ken Mihan, along with Janet Coyle, had faced a grizzly task. Carlos Da Silva had given them a ride to the hospital while they carried the flap of Nicole's leg that the shark had spat out. They had it on ice. It was freaky to them, really difficult to look at. But they knew it was their responsibility to get the tissue to the medical team without losing time. They also carried with them Nicole's ID so they could get her properly checked in.

Thinking back to that day, Ken pauses to collect his thoughts. He is clearly ruffled, irritated. "I couldn't believe it!" he finally admits. "The first thing they want at the Hospiten front desk — and by the way, this place looks like a first-class hotel, all tricked out in marble and bright lights, the works, just like a movie set — anyway, they demand seven hundred dollars for the ambulance before anything else happens. Right then and there!"

Ken hesitated at the time, reasonably sure it was illegal and unethical to deny patients care if they didn't pay immediately. But then he thought, maybe this isn't the time to stand on principle. So he handed over his credit card and paid the $700.

But matters escalated. The Hospiten staff told him they'd need $20,000 before any operation on Nicole could take place. Ken thought to himself, "You can't do that! What do you mean you won't operate unless you get the money up front? Damn it all. We've got someone dying here!"

Once again, Ken sensed how serious Nicole's situation was and decided to save fighting for another day. He contacted his credit card company, explained what was happening, and had them extend his limit to $20,000. It was an act of generosity that would eventually be reimbursed through Nicole's insurance.

We now head thousands of miles away to the cold, dark Canadian winter. Jay Moore is lying on the couch, suffering from the flu. He feels crummy. When the phone rings, his first inclination is to ignore it. Talking to anyone is the least of his desires. He just wants to hunker down and get well. But something makes him pick up the receiver. On the other end is a man he's never met: Ken Mihan. Ken introduces himself and then tries to break the news as calmly as possible. "Nicole has been attacked by a shark," he states unemotionally. "We have no details right now … other than she's in emergency surgery."

"They say the color drains from your face at times like this," Jay recalls. "Well, I could sure feel that. You know, as a policeman, I get pretty dire news from time to time. But I've never experienced anything like this. You run through Jaws-type scenarios and all you want to know is what kind of damage are we talking about? But this guy has no details at all."

Indeed, Ken is being careful not to imply that Nicole faces a life-or-death situation, just that no particulars are presently available. They talk only for a couple of minutes and then Jay hangs up. Everything seems momentarily blurry. Can this actually be happening? Can his wife, always so safe in the water, really be the victim of a shark attack? Where the hell had she been when this went down? How could her friends have let this happen to her?

Then the adrenalin kicks in. Jay knows he has to move quickly, despite the flu-induced lethargy. He gets up, calls out to his father-in-law Alberto, and shares the news.

"To say I was shocked is an understatement," Nicole's devoted father recalls. "But where was the detail? I called back twice, but this guy Ken had no update. It was incredibly frustrating. What the hell was going on down there?"

Both men realize they have to get to Cancún right away.

Jay gets on the phone to his parents, who live three hours away. He asks them to come down and pick up the kids as soon as they can. When he explains what has occurred, their reaction is, "This can't be possible!"

Alberto books into the first resort in Cancún he can find. He and his son-in-law agree that Jay will wait until his parents get there, while Alberto will leave immediately.

Twenty-four hours later Nicole's father arrives in Cancún on a flight that seems to take a lifetime. He has tried to read on the plane to distract himself from his worries, but concentrating is tough. The anguish of not knowing how gravely injured his daughter is plagues him. Worst-case scenarios play in his mind. But being the practical man that he is, Alberto remains focused on the task at hand: being there for Nicole.

Reaching the hospital, he is immediately escorted to his daughter's room. Steeling himself before entering, not sure what to expect (he still has no facts to deal with), he chooses humour as his defence. Putting a smile on his face, he enters the room. "Hi, Shark Bait!" he says gaily. It works. These are the first warm and humorous words Nicole has heard for what seems like forever and a smile breaks out on her face.

The general news they are getting at this point is that everything is okay. The consistent story is: "Serious injury. We are concerned. We think she will be able to walk. She may not have full function in her leg because she's lost muscles. As far as the arm is concerned, we are optimistic we will be able to save it. She may only have a couple of fingers that she can move, but still somewhat of a functioning hand." So, on the face of it, this seems like reasonably positive news, considering everything.

But underneath the optimism, Alberto is uneasy. He is concerned that the doctors have closed up Nicole's arm right away, without leaving time for the wounds to heal. While he recognizes these people are well-meaning, a sense that they are in over their heads begins gnawing at him.

His worries do not stop there. Because hospital visitation times are limited, Alberto finds himself with time on his hands while in Cancún. He sets out to use the hours to piece together the sequence of events and to define potential responsibility around what has befallen his daughter.

Getting an accurate picture of the timing and individuals involved proves somewhat difficult: he is confronted by language barriers, conflicting testimonies, and limited means of communication. Still, Alberto manages to create an initial, if limited, picture. Armed with this data, he tries to assess who has the onus for overseeing the safety of millions of tourists visiting Cancún every year. Not just to lay blame, but to prevent further tragedies.

"They told me resort operators were responsible for guest safety 'on the beach' up to the water's edge," he says. "But beyond that, it was the domain of the Proteccion Civil. So I contacted the local Cancún office, but didn't get very far, mostly due to language barriers. It was frustrating."

Next, Alberto contacts the Canadian consulate for assistance. He is referred to a local Mexican attorney. The ensuing conversation is disconcerting.

"I'd had previous business experience in Mexico so this was not totally surprising," he explains. "This attorney told me that any effort to pin even a limited amount of responsibility for such an event on anyone would be futile. Unlike Canada or the U.S., Mexico just doesn't have well-defined avenues of grievances, particularly for rare events like a shark attack. He told me there would be considerable 'public resistance' to any publicity and precedent-setting for a claim."

His dissatisfaction growing, Alberto points out that the only remaining avenue available to him is to work on a travel advisory. It is, in truth, an empty threat, since in his heart he does not believe that even in Canada this would be taken seriously enough to risk the opposition of a powerful travel industry. "I must have hit a nerve, though, because the lawyer got incensed and angrily accused me of trying to put hardworking Mexicans out of a job. Really? All I was doing was trying to get to the bottom of an awful circumstance that had nearly killed my daughter. What that has to do with putting people out of work I'll never know."

Related or not to Alberto's poking around, two days later Nicole receives a visit from Gloria Gebara, the Mexican secretary of tourism (*secretaría de turismo gobierno federal*), who flies in from Mexico City to extend her sympathy and wishes for a quick recovery.

It doesn't help. Nicole's pain is worsening. "I'm sure they had me sedated and on meds," she recalls, "but I still remember the throbbing, aching pain: it was through the roof. And it just kept getting worse and worse. My arm was just killing me. My whole arm up to the shoulder and then the shoulder blade … it was so intense. I've just had the fight of my life against the power and forcefulness of a shark, so I'm sure that's contributing to everything being sore. I'm dehydrated, awful headache … everything. I've got so many toxins going through my body just from the trauma itself. That will give you headaches and make you feel heavy and lethargic at the best of times. And I was just really fatigued. I was a mess. But I was alive."

Looking back, Terri Holden wasn't sure that Nicole totally understood what had happened to her at that point. She sensed her friend must have been in a state of delirium when she arrived at the hospital. When Nicole woke up in recovery and was moved to ICU, Terri reasoned she would have been in some form of shock. "Although Nicole didn't display that," she says. "Perhaps that's her nursing background coming through so she can gather herself together and deal with trauma. She's the type of person who doesn't want to let on if things are bad because she doesn't look for attention in that way."

Meanwhile, Donna Holwell, who speaks a little Spanish, tried to translate between the doctors and Nicole. Donna sensed that the hospital staff had saved her friend's life, no question. But they were not as sanitary as she'd prefer. Still, it was a pretty horrific accident and the fact that Nicole was alive was a miracle.

The sanitation remains a disquieting bugaboo to this day. Donna explains: "I remember Toni visiting Nicole and coming out saying, 'She still has sand on her feet. There's sea water. This is unacceptable.' I thought: that can't be good. You shouldn't come out of extensive surgery with sand from the beach on you. When I finally got in to see Nicole, she said, 'I'm lying in a bed of sand.' It was awful. I got the nurse to change the sandy sheet immediately. I mean, how could they have left her like that?"

Nicole's medical knowledge was playing on her too. Because the central line is an advanced type of intravenous therapy that goes directly to the heart, maintaining sterility and decreasing the risk of infection is absolutely key. But there seemed to be very little attention being paid to cleanliness. And it was driving Nicole crazy.

"As nurses, we clean all IV ports with special wipes so no bacteria is injected," she explains. "It's crucially important with these central lines to be vigilant in the cleaning process: whatever you are injecting, including any pathogens and bacteria, are introduced directly into the heart. So you have to create a sterile field and follow protocols. But these guys were doing none of that! I would cringe in fear for my wellbeing. I'd say, 'Not okay! Not okay!' hoping they'd understand. I was really, really nervous about the direct access to my heart. Sand in the sheets? Yeah, that was bad, but …"

She also worried about the deficiency of dressing changes. Nicole could not recall one even having taken place. This was clearly below the level of care that even a new nurse would administer back home.

Still, the lack of a disinfected, decontaminated approach was secondary to Nicole's horrific pain, which was worsening. She kept asking the staff if her arm and leg were okay. And they would simply peek under the bandage and say "Sí." Why were they not opening these dressings and changing them? Her bandages were already looking pretty yellowy … not a good sign.

As Nicole Moore lay in recovery in Hospiten Cancún's expensive bed, she was still trying to come to grips with what had happened to her, something so unbelievably rare. She also worried about how the impact of this event would affect her travel mates.

"I watched my dear friends come around the curtain to visit me and saw the pain on their faces. It made my heart break that I was the cause of that. I don't like to bother people, I don't like to ask for help. I'm just, 'I'm okay, I'm good, come on over here, and let me alleviate this pain *you're* feeling.' And then they'd be fine, and I knew when they walked out that they'd be okay. I answered their questions, but didn't want to tell them about my pain or anything like that. And I'm glad I could do something for them because I truly hate to hurt people or know that I'm the cause of any kind of a burden."

"She made it easier for us to deal with the trauma," says Terri. "She had a little smile on her face the moment I walked around the curtain and she just wanted a hug. She was just so happy to be alive: that's all that mattered to her at that moment. It was just sheer happiness that she was there."

"It was no effort with Nicole," says Donna. "It was so easy to be with her. I really didn't know what to say to her and I don't remember what our conversation was about. Other than she kept saying how happy she was to still be here, to be alive. I guess it was more her being so up and positive that it really lightened us. I don't know how much comfort we provided to her, but she sure provided a lot to us."

Back at home, Jay had put aside his influenza and made quick decisions about what was going to happen. Dealing with his two young daughters would be tricky, but he knew he could let his emotions kick in later. There were practical things that needed to be addressed. This is his strength: being cool under fire.

Jay decided not to tell the girls specifically what had happened. He worried that leaving the children behind full of anxiety would be wrong. Instead, he decided to explain that Mommy had had an accident and he needed to go down and help her out. He kept the details to a minimum, nothing about sharks. It worked. Tia and Ella knew they had a chance to go up and stay with their grandparents at their farm, always a good thing.

Jay was able to lean on a friend at work whose husband is a pilot for Air Canada. She could get him an immediate "buddy pass," but she'd have to fly with him. Recognizing the dire nature of the situation, she was ready whenever Jay was. Which was immediately.

And so, in the nastiest snowstorm so far that winter, they were able to get access to the "cop SUV four-by-four with snow tires" and arrived at Pearson International Airport just in time for a 7:00 a.m. flight to Cancún. By a stroke of good fortune, their plane was one of the rare trips not cancelled that day due to weather.

Jay arrived in Mexico on the second day after the shark attack. He found his wife covered up and swaddled in white blankets.

"My first reaction? I started crying, I've got to be honest," he confesses. "I couldn't overcome it. I'd wanted to be so strong for her but the emotion took over and I just gave out." He overcame his sentiments, however, and like his father-in-law's "Hi, Shark Bait," rejoinder, said to Nicole, "Okay, you can have your dog!" to which she burst into smiles. She'd been pestering her husband for some time about getting a puppy for the girls and he'd been resistant. That crumbled when he saw her. "It was so emotional. But, you know, at that point I still didn't realize the extent of what had happened. She was talking … that's all I cared about."

To the best of her ability, Nicole filled Jay in on what she understood had transpired so far. She was all wrapped up so he could see no evidence of her wounds. Typically, she had a sense of humour. Her positive, keep-moving-forward spirit kept him buoyed, despite the severity of their situation.

"I can count on one hand the number of times she'd had a bad day throughout this whole ordeal," Jay says, "where the pain is too much, or you want your old life back. If it was me, I'd be pitying myself. 'I can't do the things I want to do because of something stupid that I had no control over and it's not meant to happen and it's not as though I hopped into a race car and did something really dangerous. You don't think of going swimming as dangerous … it's not really a calculated risk!' That's what I'd be like. But Nicole? No. She was amazing!"

Meanwhile, the doctors ordered her to rest so Jay and Alberto were only allowed fifteen-minute visits. The hospital staff provided Jay with a room upstairs and offered food, while Alberto travelled back and forth to the nearby hotel he had booked.

Both men began to realize that Hospiten Cancún was a very fancy privatized hospital, dealing only with people who had money. They were also aware that the medical team had zero shark-attack experience. They didn't have a lot of confidence in the care Nicole was receiving.

On the second night of his stay in Mexico, while Nicole slept, Jay went to the Grand Park Royal Cancún Caribe. He chatted with Nicole's travel buddies and concluded they had done nothing wrong. "Not that I had doubts about that," he recalls, "but it's human nature to want to hold someone responsible. In the end, all I could do was blame a shark!"

"Poor Jay was a basket case," says Cyndi. "His whole world had just been turned upside down. The lack of sleep was evident, trying to cope with his children and travelling down here to be with his wife. He'd been sick. He was in a daze. The poor guy, I really felt for him."

But Jay knew one thing for certain: he had to get Nicole home. Pronto!

8

Adiós Cancún!

February 3

Nicole was worried. She was in severe pain and it was worsening.

Jay and Alberto were beyond concerned.

Neither Nicole's arm nor her leg were improving in any way. In fact, she could tell that her limbs were declining in strength and resiliency.

And Dr. Rafael Velasco seemed to be absent. They requested his presence, only to be told he was in Mexico City. They insisted he return immediately.

Nicole was happy to see the doctor when he got back. She needed someone senior to tell her what was going on, someone to take control of things.

Velasco opened up the bandages. For the first time, Nicole got a look at her arm.

"It was a mess. It was gross," she explains. "Then I gazed up at him and saw this look on his face that said it all. It was just a look of 'Oh!' It was not a look of confidence, not the sense of optimism and hope you want from your doctor."

Velasco closed up the bandage and said, almost to himself, "Home." He then addressed Nicole, "We've done all we can do for you here. It's fine ... not as good as we'd hoped but it's time for you to go home. We'll give you the medical clearance. You can move to the medical floor now and start making arrangements."

All Nicole heard was "home" and she was happy. Still, she worried that the look on the doctor's face spoke volumes: He seemed to accept it was not right, but he didn't know what to do other than send Nicole back to Canada.

On day four, Nicole was moved from intensive care onto the main medical floor. They set it up so Jay could be in the room with her in his own bed. They received real food in an attractive setting.

Creature comforts taken care of, Jay and Alberto started getting the insurance program into effect to ease their way home.

This was a time of major frustration. Jay contacted the insurance company, explained the unusual circumstances they faced, and said they needed to get Nicole back to Toronto immediately. Day four went by with no word from the insurance company. Day five: still no answer.

Jay pressed on, looking for any and all opportunities to fly Nicole home and into the care she deserved. And badly needed. He could get no straight answers from the insurance company as to why they could not locate a hospital to accept her. All they came back to him with was, "No bed, no doctor." In *all* of Ontario, there's no bed? There's no doctor? It seemed incomprehensible to him. They told him it would take at least three days to find somewhere. That obviously wasn't going to work.

Alberto appealed to the Canadian consulate, but they were unable to help. His frustration and impatience grew.

While this was going on, Nicole was attempting to deal with calls from the media and family members who were contacting her for updates. Meanwhile, the pain she endured was extreme, almost unbearable.

Then Jay got a brainwave. He placed a call to his mother, Becky, who works at a hospital in northern Ontario. Could she help? Wasting no time, Becky called Dr. Olayiwola Kassim, a world-renowned pathologist for whom she acted as personal assistant. She found him at a social function, but he took her call, listened patiently, and committed to seeing what he could do when he returned home later that night.

"Dr. Kassim is this big, intimidating Nigerian man who's six and a half feet tall," says Nicole. "I'd met him previously because I'd sat in on some of his autopsies, being the curious nurse I am. But underneath that imposing exterior is a soft teddy bear who's super friendly. And the fact is, Becky's plea weighed heavily on him: he had a gut feeling this was a predicament that shouldn't wait. So he left the festivities, returned home, and got to work. He does these kinds of things for people all over the world — a true giver."

Dr. Kassim's goal was to find the best place for Nicole, then learn who was the top team at that hospital. He contacted Dr. Laura Snell at the Sunnybrook Health Sciences Centre in Toronto. He confessed he didn't know her, but he knew of her. It was a chance.

When his call finally went through, it was an exhausted Laura Snell who picked up. She had been on call since the Monday night of that week. It was her February week of call — really busy, non-stop. Laura had been up all night, every night, operating. It doesn't always happen that way, but every now and then she'd get a week where it seemed like a disaster. To compound matters, she had an eight-month-old baby at home. She'd had no opportunity to even watch the news, so she didn't know what was going on in the world. It was as though she'd been completely shut off in her own space that week, just trying to keep up with all the referrals.

"I'd been up all night Monday, Tuesday, Wednesday, Thursday, and I was so tired and my pager just didn't stop going off all week," Laura recalls. "So at about midnight on the Friday — I remember this so clearly now — I had just arrived home, dead tired. Suddenly the beeper goes and it's this pathologist from somewhere. I had no idea who he was, no clue. He just says, 'I'm doctor so and so. I have this young nurse and she's almost the same age as you and she's been attacked by a shark and she really needs to be transferred back to Canada. Will you accept her care?' I was too tired to even figure out where he was calling from."

Normally Dr. Snell would hang up the phone, call Sunnybrook, and see if there were any beds, then she'd call the trauma team and let them know to get involved. Typically there are no beds so she would just say "no." But in this unusual instance, she was just too tired to do any of that. So she simply said, "Sure." That was it. She was just too exhausted to go through the usual protocols. All she'd heard was "… young person, shark attack, a wound on her leg…." And so she reasoned it was probably just a tiny thing. There was no mention of the patient's arm at all.

"I just wanted to go to sleep. I didn't want to call all these people. Actually, I did contact the floor and they said they had one female bed open, and I said, 'Snag it because there's a nurse that's coming' and whatever … and then I went to sleep. I wouldn't hear anything more for twenty-four hours."

On the morning of February 5 — day six of the ordeal — Jay immediately called the insurance company and explained he had taken care of business himself, doing what he felt they should be doing: earning their premiums by finding a hospital, a bed, and a doctor for his wife who was dealing with life-threatening conditions. All the insurers had to do now was organize a medical jet for the next day.

The confirmation came back that a plane would be there by 1:30 p.m. that day.

The sense of relief was profound. With concerns about how the patient was being treated medically in Cancún, the need to get her back to Canada and into more familiar care was intense. Nicole, Jay, and Alberto sighed and relaxed. But only slightly.

As they prepared to leave — Nicole and Jay via the air ambulance and Alberto by a commercial flight — Nicole was told she would have to revisit the operating room before leaving. The staff wished to insert a chest tube, because her lung was apparently collapsing by 30 percent on her right side. They didn't want her to fly without re-inflating the lung. An unexpected, unscheduled one-hour operation occurred. Not for the first time, Nicole thought back to the struggle the team had experienced trying to install the central line into her heart. She wondered again if they had nicked her lung in the process.

A second unusual occurrence arose when they handed her an envelope containing the operation report that was supposed to detail Nicole's medical records. She was thankful at the time, but later discovered that the meagre document's two virtually meaningless paragraphs were completely insufficient.

This document — and the inability to retrieve anything more detailed from Hospiten Cancún — was what would later lead to thoughts of a cover up.

* * *

JET I.C.U. is an accredited international air ambulance operator specializing in emergency medical flights to and from anywhere in the world. They work out of Brooksville, Florida, where the company boasts its own medical staff, pilots, ground crew, and operations centre. They fly specially designed, fully equipped LearJets — airborne intensive care units outfitted to get patients with acute medical issues to help quickly, providing the capacity to cruise at altitudes of 45,000 feet and at speeds in excess of 500 miles per hour, ensuring patient comfort high above adverse weather conditions.

On the morning of February 5, 2011, Paul Addlestone, a JET I.C.U. on-duty flight nurse/paramedic, received a phone call at his home in

Courtesy of Paul Addlestone

Paul Addlestone.

Tampa Bay. He was told to be at the hangar, ready to leave for Cancún in ninety minutes. Given the regular one-hour and twenty-minute drive to get there, the forty-two-year-old, originally from Leister, England, knew there was no time to lose.

On arriving at the hangar, all he had was a report saying that they were to pick up a female in Cancún with multiple shark bites to her lower and upper extremities. They had no experience caring for victims of shark attacks. But they did regularly deal with everything from gunshots to strokes to cancer patients to pulmonary embolisms — ailments that really run the gamut.

Less than two hours later, the JET I.C.U. Lear 25D touched down at Cancún International, one of the busiest airports in the Caribbean, the point of entry for fun lovers headed to the "Mundo Maya." It is a facility that seems to have been under construction forever. Avoiding the main terminal, the pilot taxied to the FBO facility used mainly for chartered flights and private planes. There, the pilot, co-pilot, and two medical crew (Paul and another paramedic) found an ambulance waiting for them on the tarmac. After clearing customs, they headed over to greet Nicole Moore.

From their initial contact, they found her to be in good spirits, fit to fly, awake, and talking coherently. Significant bandaging on her body suggested major injuries, but the bleeding appeared to be controlled, despite an elevated white count and hemoglobin a little on the low side.

Paul Addlestone was not surprised to receive sketchy medical records. He'd always felt there was a sparseness of information emerging from hospital facilities at vacation destinations in Mexico. "Whatever they gave us we handed over in Canada when we arrived. We didn't have time to review surgical reports, but it seemed all they had done was an initial … what appeared to be a clamping of the vessels and sort of irrigating and cleaning out the wound a bit. But it turns out they did a terrible job with that. Certainly they didn't meet the 'industry standards' we rely on in North America."

Paul didn't actually see the extent of Nicole's injuries until they arrived in Toronto. "It's not my job to risk causing arterial bleeding if I open up wounds on the plane, nor should I second guess the physician and say, 'You need to fix this!'

"I don't want to dis anyone," he adds, "but the lack of information and the type of care she received is typical of places like Cancún. God forbid, if you were going to have a medical issue, you'd be more comfortable with the level of care you'd receive in Europe and North America, versus a small resort town in Mexico. I mean, it may be good care for Mexico or for that kind of area, but in Nicole's case what became evident when we got her to Canada was that it didn't look they'd really done anything."

The four-and-a-half hour flight was uneventful and included a brief stop for refuelling in Jacksonville. The crew was astonished at Nicole's good spirits and took the opportunity to keep her from being stressed. "She's an amazing person; you see this after spending five minutes with her," says Paul. "Still, we reminded her to look on the bright side. 'You're alive, you may or may not lose an arm, but you're going to be there for your kids.' It was pretty amazing. She and her husband took it really well. It was pretty evident they were both ecstatic to have us get them out of Cancún because their experience in the Mexican hospital had not been the best."

Paul and his associate treated Nicole for pain with intravenous medications. And thankfully, their patient, being a registered nurse, could fill in some blanks about what had occurred. The fact that she appeared relaxed, even cracking jokes, reduced the pressure.

The Lear 25D made its way north, where the daylight surrendered to darkness. Landing in Toronto, they were greeted by a foot and a half of newly fallen snow. The jet crew members were told they would have to wait for customs officers to arrive to clear the group's entry into Canada. They took Nicole's gurney from the plane and set it down in the snow and waited.

And waited. And waited. And waited.

Finally, the pilot called customs again. They were now told that weather-oriented traffic was holding up their officer and delaying his arrival at the airport. The pilot stressed the need to move quickly. "This is getting really serious," he said

"Okay, just tell them to go," the representative finally said.

And so Nicole and Jay entered their home and native land without the authority of the Canadian Border Services Agency.

Next stop: Sunnybrook.

9

Struggle for Survival: Canada

Sunnybrook Health Sciences Centre sits within a stone's throw of one of Toronto's wealthiest neighbourhoods. The hospital lies at the edge of a grand park-like setting, comprising gently rolling hills, ravines, walking and riding trails, and meandering streams. Opened in 1948 as Canada's

Sunnybrook Hospital

Sunnybrook Health Sciences Centre.

largest medical facility for military veterans, Sunnybrook stands as the symbol of a nation's gratitude to its war participants. It is also a fully affiliated University of Toronto teaching facility, serving the general public.

In 1976 the hospital was established as the country's first regional trauma unit to care for those people sustaining life-threatening multiple injuries. This was Nicole Moore's classification when she arrived on that cold, snowy February night. While the trauma unit regularly deals with a spectrum of wounds from motor vehicle accidents to pedestrian falls and even gang-related offences, the fact that the nearest warm seawater is 2,500 miles away means a shark-attack victim darkening their doorstep is … well … as rare as a shark attack.

Nicole had done a student rotation at Sunnybrook years before, while training as a nurse. After the uncertainty of the hospital in Mexico, she felt relieved to be in such familiar settings.

"I had just started to work on my own after partnering with a senior nurse for training at Sunnybrook," says Hasumie Hosogoe, a nurse of Japanese and Finnish heritage, age twenty-seven at the time. "I was fresh on my own. And as a nurse, to receive someone from Mexico who had been attacked by a shark … omigosh, I just found that to be overwhelming. It was very intimidating. I was asking myself, 'Can I take this patient on?'"

Jay Clavio, age twenty-six, had no doubts. Having worked as a nurse at Sunnybrook for three years, he knew how unusual it was to receive a patient who'd experienced a shark assault. It was the first time he'd ever heard of such a thing, but he was intrigued. Although he wasn't assigned to Nicole right away, he wanted to be on that case. It would be Hasumie and Jay who helped Nicole survive over the next few months.

Hasumie was the receiving health care worker, the first person Nicole met at Sunnybrook. Hasumie could see Nicole's fingers on her bandaged arm, and was concerned that they didn't look very healthy. Some were blue, some completely black. She sensed Nicole was very nervous about this. Hasumie found the situation upsetting.

"Her injuries were probably the most severe I'd ever seen in my nursing career," says Jay Clavio. "And yet, her attitude was like that of someone who's just walked into the hospital and is complaining of something very minimal. She has the strongest will I've ever come across from a human being, absolutely."

Both Hasumie and Jay were a little intimidated that Nicole was a nurse, especially since they were both relatively new to the profession. Hasumie admitted to being cautious, a little slow, but stressed that she would not miss any steps. Jay worried their patient might be picky about her care, needing to control what was happening. It turned out they had nothing to be concerned about. Nicole was welcoming, calm, and helpful, even taking the role of a mentor, offering tips on dressing changes and how to do certain types of bandaging. Both nurses confessed later they had grown professionally from having this bright woman as a patient.

Still, Nicole Moore needed a heroine in her life just then. And Dr. Laura Snell was the woman of the hour.

Sunnybrook Hospital

Dr. Laura Snell.

Laura is that kind of person you might call "cute as a button." Indeed, she could pass for ten years younger than her age of thirty-six, despite being the mother of two youngsters. But don't be fooled by her appearance. Dr. Snell is a highly respected specialist in Sunnybrook's division of plastic and reconstructive surgery. Her focus is on oncologic ablative defects, particularly breast reconstruction. She is a graduate of the Western University medical school and the plastic surgery residency program at the University of Toronto. In addition, she pursued a microvascular and reconstructive surgery fellowship at Memorial Sloan Kettering Cancer Center in New York City and holds a master's of science in biostatistics from Columbia University. She was also the recipient of the prestigious Ross Tilley Scholarship for plastic and reconstructive surgery by the Canadian Society of Plastic Surgeons.

Dr. Snell had been operating all day on that Saturday when, at 10:00 p.m., she got a call saying her patient had arrived, complete with a chest tube and big dressings on her arm and leg. Her immediate reaction was *What patient are you talking about?* She'd forgotten that she'd accepted this case twenty-four hours earlier in a state of exhaustion. But then she recalled the late-night commitment she'd made to the doctor with the strange name whom she didn't even know. Laura shook her head, straightened her attire, and went to see Nicole. It only took one glance to realize the severity of what she had agreed to take on. *Have I made a mistake?* she whispered quietly to herself.

When asked if she'd ever been confronted by the victim of a shark attack, Dr. Snell smiles and admits that Nicole Moore's arrival at Sunnybrook that night broke new ground for her. Yet she is quick to point out that she deals regularly with major wounds. Ultimately, whether the injury comes from an encounter with a machine or an animal, it's still a laceration trauma that needs to be dealt with. This scope of injury and magnitude of wound were similar to what the trauma team sees in other cases. Still, it *was* a shark attack.

"Yes, I'm famous for this case now amongst my plastic surgery colleagues," says Dr. Snell, "and that's because of the shark. It's a dramatic type of case. But at the time, it was just 'follow the regular protocols.'"

Joining Dr. Snell was twenty-seven-year-old Dr. Andrew Fagan. Schooled at Memorial University in St. John's, Newfoundland, the tall, self-confessed "surfer dude" with wavy brown hair had developed an interest in plastic surgery and moved west to start his residency at Sunnybrook. As an "ocean boy," used to surfing regularly in the north Atlantic, he had a special interest in Nicole's case.

"What amazed us was seeing teeth marks on her bones," Dr. Fagan recalled. "I mean, that beast was incredibly powerful! And there was also the fact that if the shark had bitten any closer to the big sciatic nerve in her leg, just a fraction of an inch away, she never would have been able to pull herself out of the water. She literally would not have been able to stand up. And if the shark had nicked her femoral artery… well, it's pretty clear, she would have drowned or been dragged out to sea right then and there."

Hasumie was unsure just how well Nicole had been cared for in Cancún. "When she came in with a chest tube that was strange, because it means there is a blood issue or accumulation of air in the lungs. But knowing that it was only her limbs that got damaged, it seemed questionable to me what had happened. And because there were no medical records to speak of … it struck me as odd."

"I can't speculate," Dr. Snell comments about what may have occurred in the Hospiten Cancún. She is cautious, uncomfortable criticizing fellow professionals. Yet she is clearly rattled by what she perceives as questionable practices. Nicole had an obvious compartment syndrome (a limb- and life-threatening condition that occurs where there is insufficient blood supply to the muscles and nerves, often leading to nerve damage). "Whether this had developed in the course of a few hours or a few days, I don't know," Dr. Snell says. "Nicole had poor circulation to her arm and hand and how long it had been like that I can't say. She definitely had sutures in her forearm so they had operated on her at some point. And there had been at least one dressing change. Same thing with her leg. But we had no records to rely on, so who knew?"

What Laura did know was that she had a patient who was in serious trouble. Removing the bandages, seeing the decay and still-present seawater and sand convinced her she needed to get into an operating room immediately. The smell of pus and exudate was overwhelming. The fact that the flap attached to Nicole's leg had no blood supply and was simply rotting away was shocking. And the discoloured fingers did not bode at all well for saving her arm. Dr. Snell ordered up an OR on a STAT basis.

"I remember Laura being calm and saying, 'Let's see what we've got,'" says Nicole. "So she pulls back the bandage on my leg first, and all this stuff just oozes out, horrible green discharge, terrible smelling. I just looked at her and said, 'Oh, that's wrong.' And she said, 'Yeah, that's really wrong.' And she closed it back up."

Then Dr. Snell opened the dressings on Nicole's arm. The rotten smell caught them both off guard. Laura didn't say too much, she just looked at the wounds, seemingly with horror: emaciated, wet tissue that was swollen and necrotic with a lot of black pieces. Fingers that were definitely black, oozing puss, dirty … the bandages were filthy. Nicole felt it had been five days since they'd put those bandages on back in Mexico. She still could not recall *any* dressing changes after the initial operation. That was pretty much confirmed because in the OR Dr. Snell washed out sand and debris.

Paul Addlestone had accompanied Nicole from the airport to the hospital, and waited around to ensure she was in good hands. Before leaving, he attended while Dr. Snell uncovered her wounds. "It was green and there was pus and quite a bit of discharge," he recalls. "There was still sand in the wounds. They hadn't been irrigated well. They were still filthy. It didn't really look like they'd done anything in Mexico."

Moving to the operating room, the team put Nicole to sleep so they could have a detailed look at her status. They debrided the wounds, removing dead, damaged, and infected tissue, foreign bodies, and sutures.

"These were more extensive wounds than I had thought, given what I had been told on the phone," says Dr. Snell. "That being said, the principle of the wounds was not more extensive than what we see with other injuries … it wasn't something we haven't dealt with before, just a different cause."

Dr. Snell was no longer able to ignore what she had felt best keeping to herself until that point: it was unlikely that they would be able to salvage Nicole's arm. There was no blood supply past the point where most of the injury was, there was no circulation, and it was apparent there had been no blood flow within the arm for some time.

Dr. Snell also knew that her patient's leg was going to require many, many surgeries to save, if they could do that at all. Dr. Fagan was less optimistic. "Frankly, I was very concerned she was going to have her arm amputated, but part of me thought we'd end up disarticulating her leg at her hip joint as well. Losing an arm *and* a leg: well, that would be just overwhelming to anyone."

Dr. Snell was pretty sure Nicole was already septic — a medical condition resulting from severe infection, which can be lethal. Sunnybrook's Infectious Disease Service was called into action. They were intent on isolating her and treating her for absolutely everything that could be a contaminant by using high doses of mega-antibiotics.

What the medical team recognized was that animal bites are considerably worse than, say, knife wounds. A shark's mouth is a nest of bacterial growth. Nicole received deep bites from an animal with known pathogens, in the ocean, which carries other germs. Then she was yanked onto a beach and rolled in the sand, and finally she headed off to a hospital in Mexico where there was no evidence that any actions at all were taken to sterilize her.

Septic patients who get that kind of infection don't tend to survive very often or for very long. Once the body starts to generate an inflammatory response to an infection it can be difficult to recover from. Infection is one of the big killers in hospitals.

Nicole knew this and it worried her.

The truth was, Nicole was pretty close to death from the infections in her leg, arm, and hand. "You are lucky to have returned to Canada when you did," she was told, "because you were very close to heading down that road. If you had arrived twenty-four to forty-eight hours later, you wouldn't be here. You'd be dead."

If you're not used to medical photographs, you need to be prepared for what you're about to see: actual photographs of Nicole Moore's wounds. Ever wondered what a shark could do to you? Here's your answer …

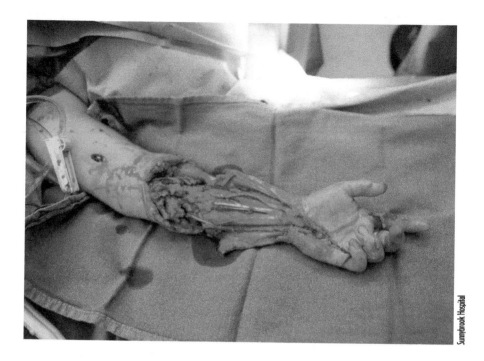

Sunnybrook Hospital

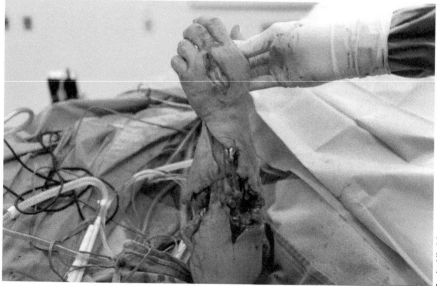

Sunnybrook Hospital

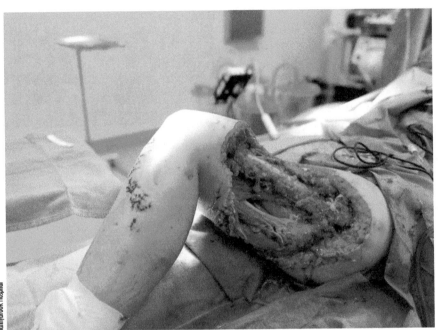

Over the next few hours the medical team conducted procedures to discover what live tissue remained. They removed the dead flap the Mexicans had sutured onto Nicole's leg and replaced this with a large dressing.

"The tissue flap on her thigh had been just stapled in place," Dr. Snell comments. "But that is not a principle of care we would follow here. Microsurgery involves taking a piece of tissue from one part of the body and putting it onto another. You can't get a piece of tissue like that to survive just by sticking it on. You actually have to use a microscope and sew blood vessels together, and you would only do that with clean tissue, not something that had been contaminated by being in the ocean and in a shark's mouth. So it seemed kind of strange. I couldn't imagine why they had done that in Mexico. The other thing we don't like in plastics is dead space: you need all the tissues to be touching in order for blood vessels to grow and for things to heal together. But here we had a piece of tissue tented across and then there was all this dead space underneath. Whether that had developed over the course of a few days I have no idea, but it's not an approach we would ever use here."

Dr. Snell began releasing all of the sutures in Nicole's left arm in order to relieve some of the pressure. She was quickly able to see a significant amount of necrotic tissue. The medical team tried to determine blood flow, and cut open her forearm because the compartment syndrome was causing all of the tissue to swell. They applied fasciotomy, a surgical procedure used to relieve tension or pressure, in order to treat the resulting loss of circulation to the area of tissue and muscle.

Following this first explorative surgery, early in the morning of February 6, Dr. Snell felt she should meet with Nicole's husband.

"I'd been just sitting there waiting," Jay recalls. "Then Laura comes in around five a.m. and tells me the injuries are more extensive than anyone had thought and that they would require more debridement procedures in order to determine next steps." She also told Jay she was guardedly optimistic. But she again chose to remain silent on her concern about the potential inability to salvage Nicole's arm.

Jay felt Dr. Snell was frustrated because she didn't have records. He also had the feeling that she did not understand why the Mexican team had done what they did. Even if they had no experience with a shark bite or any animal bite, he knew that basic medical expertise said you don't close a wound like that: you go back in and you clean it out. But they didn't do that. Why? It was so obviously infected. Why didn't they adequately wash it out? And as for the arm: with any fresh injury or broken bone, you never close the wound since it causes compartment syndrome. That's medicine 101. Jay thought that Dr. Snell sensed a whole bunch of wrongdoing, things any physician should know about or act on, but in Mexico this simply hadn't been done.

"At this point, I think I was in shock in terms of 'this is crazy.' And then the whirlwind began from that day forward," Jay says.

Dr. Snell, clearly exhausted, talked next with Nicole. "'Here's all the wrong stuff I found,' she told me," Nicole recalls. "'You're in bad shape. You're not presenting but I can't believe how well you're sitting up and talking: you should be really, really ill. It took litres of saline to wash out the wounds, just to even get rid of the sand and debris.' She added that this is just not acceptable in medicine."

At the same time, Dr. Snell found Nicole to be extremely positive and open, keen to know everything, ready to move forward. "She never seemed very surprised by what I told her. It was always, 'Okay, what do we do next?'"

"Next" came forty-eight hours later, when Dr. Snell restarted the debridement so that she could take a second look.

Meanwhile, Jay's parents, Reg and Becky Moore, had been instrumental in trying to maintain a sense of normalcy in the lives of the two children, Tia and Ella. The girls' mom had been savagely attacked by a shark and she'd been hospitalized for a long time. That could really mess up a kid. But without hesitation or regard for their own responsibilities, Nicole's in-laws put their busy lives on hold and set their focus on their granddaughters' well being. Often making the five-hundred-kilometre round trip just to pick up or drop off the kids, they set out to surround them with a fun and nurturing environment during such a fragile time.

"I knew that the girls were in good hands," says Nicole, "and that if either Tia or Ella were showing signs of suffering, they would be looked after, and I would know about it. But amazingly, the kids were fine throughout." (Perhaps not so amazingly when you realize they come from Nicole!)

"It turns out the most traumatic part for the kids was having to come home from grandma and grandpa's," laughs Jay. "I think they would gladly move up there and just visit us if they could."

"I'm lucky to have the best in-laws in the world." Nicole beams with a bright smile. "No monster-in-laws here! I have a deep love and respect for them and I'm so grateful for what they've done."

So it was that on a cold, snowy day in February, Jay's parents made the long trek and brought Tia and Ella to visit their mom for the first time. The thoughtful staff covered Nicole up, so her daughters would not see her wounds. "I was worried they'd cry or not want to see me or it would be too traumatic for them," says Nicole. "But it worked out great. They walked in and it was 'Mommmmmy!' with big hugs. Within an hour they were in bed with me snuggling."

From a medical perspective, however, Nicole was far from out of the woods.

Her hemoglobin count was seventy-three (one hundred sixty is normal), meaning she was anemic — critically anemic — because she was missing so many red blood cells, the result of losing so much blood. They started pumping units of blood into her, but her hemoglobin wasn't going up. Why?

Dr. Snell was also concerned that a large portion of Nicole's femur, the longest, strongest bone in the body, was exposed. "Often in principal wound care," she explains, "if you have a large area of bone that is open without having vascular coverage, there is a significant risk of osteomyelitis — infection and inflammation of the bone or bone marrow. So I conferred with my colleagues, who agreed that sooner rather than later we should bring her to the operating room for a free tissue transfer to cover the bone: a 'free flap.'"

Essentially, this meant taking donor tissue from elsewhere on Nicole's body and hooking it up to blood vessels, then covering the bone. It would not be a simple procedure.

10

A Portrait of Courage

At Sunnybrook, day six post-op became known as the Date of Defeat. On February 8, Nicole returned to the OR for the third time so her doctors could attempt to cover her exposed femur. The free-flap procedure involved a ten-hour operation wherein Dr. Snell had two surgeons working by her side.

"One of my colleagues is an upper limb specialist so he was managing Nicole's hand," Dr. Snell explains. "It's always good to have two opinions. So we did the free-flap surgery, taking tissue from one leg to cover the bone — essentially harvesting tissue from her right thigh to cover her left thigh. We were taking the skin and the fat, a skin graft, just a thin shaving, and putting that on the donor site and then taking the thick tissue and moving it to the other side. But thick tissue can't survive like a shaving of skin can unless it has a blood supply. So you get the microscope and you find an artery and a vein and you connect the two in order for it to get its own circulation."

Everyone — from the surgical team to the nurses to Nicole herself — seemed pleased with the outcome. Still, they knew that if a flap like this is going to reject, it would do so in twenty-four to forty-eight hours. Like any organ replacement, the body either takes it or discards it. In order to prevent the rejection, there is a strict routine: the patient is encouraged not to move and stay in bed, like a statue.

Nicole was compliant.

The countdown began.

By day three hopes were high, and everyone felt relieved to be in safe waters.

Day four came and went.

So did day five.

But then day six arrived.

"It seemed every two hours they were checking the flap," recalls Nicole. "Then every four hours. And this goes on for days until we're way past the danger zone. But then, one time Jay Clavio comes in and he's obviously upset and I hear him say, 'You must be kidding! I must be doing this wrong.' Right away, I knew something was not right. And then Laura comes in and says, 'I can't believe this' and starts removing staples and cutting in to see if there is blood response."

But there was none.

Laura: "One of the residents said to me, 'Something just looks funny.' There was an arterial pulse at the flap, which was good, but he said, 'It looks strange. It feels cool, it just doesn't look like it did yesterday.' So I went up immediately and saw that at this late stage, something wasn't right. You could still hear the pulsation in the scope but it had changed. So we immediately brought Nicole back to the operating room and spent a few hours trying to salvage the flap."

But for all their efforts, the doctors had to face a disquieting fact: the operation had failed. Day six was the date of defeat.

"I have to tell you, I was absolutely devastated," says Laura. "The flap had been so beautiful, it was perfect, the contour was great, Nicole was doing really well ... but then it was so shocking what happened."

"I remember that morning as clear as if it were yesterday," recalls Andrew Fagan. "It was one of the worst days of my medical career: a sinking feeling that this woman has been through so much, has endured so well, she's such a good person ... and this thing has screwed up. It's just not fair! I'd come to know Nicole well, I'd met her husband — one of the nicest guys I've ever met; he was a huge support to her all along — I'd seen pictures of her kids, heard stories about the children, met her father ... they're all such great people. And I just can't believe this is happening to this woman. And we organize the OR and I'm holding her hand when she goes in and she asks me to hold her hand again when she's being put under ... and I still can't believe that this is happening to her...." Dr. Fagan pauses for a moment. His normal reliable resolve has been battered. He finally admits, "It's one of those few instances where I went home after work and called my mother and said, 'Mom I need to unwind on someone. I need to download what's going on because it's just been a terrible day.'"

He wasn't alone. For the only time during her long Sunnybrook stay, the bad news finally broke Nicole Moore's spirit.

"I was devastated, crushed. I mean, even Dr. Snell was in tears. And I just thought, *Can anything else go wrong?* Let me have something positive because it's all been one step forward, two steps back, both here and in Mexico! Just as we gain something, there's something else lost! Yet another challenge. But this was such a big win of mine: I was showing everybody my leg. It gave me something positive to hold onto for a few days, and it was great. But guess what: let's take that away from me too! I felt cheated. I felt *Why did this go wrong, why did this happen? Can't anything go right for me? When is this going to stop? Why can't I be with my children?* That, and now I've got a new wound on my right leg so I'm worse off than I was before!"

As Nicole took stock, she realized they were back to where she was when they came in from Mexico. Her arm was still open. In fact, it was worsening. Her leg had a gaping wound, the bone still exposed. They didn't know how bad her infections were. And her pain — it's safe to say that no one should be made to endure such pain.

"I broke," Nicole says with misty eyes. "I had a hissy fit. I just bawled. I just cried and cried. And I said, 'I don't want visitors anymore. Just piss off and leave me alone!'"

What's worse is that it was February 14, Valentine's Day, an occasion for celebrating love, not loss. It was a vulnerable time for Nicole. Her late mother's birthday was on February 16. She had died on the 18th. "It was just a bad time, my first real crash," Nicole admits. "I was destroyed, sad and emotional, but I felt I was entitled to feel that way so I just let it happen. For the rest of that day, I just felt, 'Screw you! I'm so blue, I'm so sad.'"

Those around her were alarmed to see Nicole collapse in this way, yet they felt helpless. She seemed to languish in her self-imposed "pity party." All bystanders could do was recognize the need for this breakdown ... and wait.

But then something happened that would prove to be just the remedy she needed. And it came as a revelation to her. Slowly, gradually, between tears, Nicole grasped her laptop. She began keying in with one hand just what had happened. She entered her emotions into the blog a friend had initiated for her, typing away as a form of therapy. She and Jay spent the rest of the day quietly.

Bad Day

Posted on February 14, 2011 by Nicole Moore

Morning all. Today is a bad day. My leg had developed a complication and they are taking me to the OR shortly. I likely will not be on the blog for the rest of the day so I wanted to apologize if you post something and it does not make it up on the blog today but please keep the comments coming.

I love them. Keep those prayers coming too as I really need them today.

I'll let you all know how I'm doing when I can.

The next morning Nicole awoke with a heavy heart, left over from the day before. She tried giving herself the usual personal pep talk, but as much as she needed to bolster her normally reliable mental fortitude, her heart just wasn't onboard. At least not until she opened her blog.

"I was absolutely blown away by the responses," she explains, reacting with a sense of awe. "I mean, here I am getting comments from people I'd never even met who were following my progress on the Internet. At a time when I couldn't support myself, here were people propping me up, bracing me, encouraging me, telling me to keep fighting the good fight. It's amazing how they just picked me up. When I couldn't carry myself, it was other people who lifted me up. And you know what? If anyone reading this doesn't think you can make a difference, forget that: you *can* make a difference. I knew I felt very loved and very supported. Caring can move mountains. Without a sense of care, there is no community. I tell people, 'Care for someone every day.' And I mean it."

And so she rebounded as only Nicole can, telling a surprised Jay Clavio, "Today is a new day. I feel like crap, but chin up and let's keep moving forward."

As for why the flap was rejected, to this day the jury is still out. Dr. Snell has gone to various colleges and written to other plastics centres seeking opinions. One theory is that Nicole's body had lost the periosteum (the membrane around the bone that muscles can attach onto) so the flap may have had nothing significant enough to adhere to. Another hypothesis is that her body was still experiencing too much shock to allow for healing after all she had endured. Everyone agreed that Nicole was at a high risk for rejection for twenty-four to forty-eight hours — but to have it fail after six days?

Laura and Andrew talked and talked about this at length. They looked at everything. They asked themselves why, in spite of two previous debridements and another at the beginning of that surgery, was the flap rejected? Was the wound not 100 percent clean at the time of the free flap going down? It certainly looked clean. All the tissue beds looked viable. The bone looked good. Vessels looked patent. For the first five days the free flap was flowing beautifully.

Another possibility they considered was the size and anatomy of the wound that they were covering with the free flap. The operating team had to place the vessels in a position where they were spanning a hard section of bone, ensuring they weren't under tension. They splint Nicole's leg and bandaged it in such a way that there was a big, bulky dressing. But they didn't want to put her leg in a rigid position where she couldn't move it at all. So if her leg rotated, even slightly, could these small vessels have been put under a slight increase in tension, resulting in a thrombosis of the artery?

Nonetheless, what had occurred couldn't be reversed. It was time to look ahead, which meant hospital rest for Nicole, followed by weekly operations and continual debridements of her arm and leg. It just seemed to go on and on.

Now, even the most dire medical situations have moments of comic relief. In this case it was the "shark hat" incident.

Andrew Fagan explains: "This was bad! It was probably the most ill-conceived time to wear that hat. Anyway, here's what went down. It was such an emotionally charged morning because we really wanted that free flap to survive, so we're moving quickly to see if we could save it. And I just grabbed a scrub cap that an old mentor of mine had given me. It had these huge fish on it but I didn't notice. And here's me holding Nicole's hand as we hurry down to the OR and then I'm holding her hand again as they do the anesthetic and all the while, there's this big, bloody shark on my forehead! And I'm staring at her, trying to talk to her calmly, saying everything is going to be all right, and we're going to take the best care of you that we can, that sort of thing. And I can only imagine what she is thinking of me, looking at this big shark plastered in the middle of my forehead. Man, I'm glad she took that with a sense of humour because it could have gone the other way!

"Laura came up to me afterward and said, 'Do you realize what you have on your head?'

"And I took it off and I'm just like, 'I am such an idiot!'

"Ahhh, the life of a sleep-deprived surgery resident!"

Meanwhile, being bedridden all that time had left Nicole susceptible to bedsores. Dr. Snell insisted her patient have a special mechanical mattress that pumps air and fluctuates the pressure in the bed, improving comfort and decreasing her risk of bedsores, helping with her recovery. But one day, while Nicole was on strict instructions not to move, the bed company came to collect this special mattress while she was still on it. Nicole was the most expensive patient on the floor and the unit manager wanted to control costs. It was chaos. Despite the "No Movement" orders, Nicole was placed onto a regular mattress. Within a day, her fragile skin was suffering.

Dr. Snell wasn't going to let that happen on her watch! She got angry at the hospital administrator and, with some additional help from Nicole's protective and persuasive father, the bed was soon returned.

In the midst of this rough time, unrewarding for the patient, doctors, nurses, and family members, there was a special something that kept Nicole going: her environment. The room she lived in was covered wall-to-wall with photos, scrapbook pages from her kids, cards, angels, and lots of art. One friend had even brought a huge container of candy sharks and it became a little ritual: you had to eat or attack one of these sharks when you came to visit.

Helping to cover the bleak view of a brick wall from her hospital window was an antique frame containing a stained-glass image of a tree. Created by her sister-in-law, the piece served to change Nicole's perspective, revising her view and acting as a symbolic part of her recovery.

"People gave me all sorts of things to help brighten my days and show support," she recalls. "Their thoughtfulness and caring touched me very deeply."

11

Confronting Reality: Amputation

Life went on. The surgeons' focus went back and forth, one day the arm, the next the leg. Accepting that there was no clear explanation for why the free-flap process had failed, Dr. Snell knew that her Plan B would have to create some coverage over the bone and get Nicole up and walking. But that just wasn't possible right then. Her leg needed time to heal. So on February 22 they did a tissue transplant and a placed a specialized vacuum dressing on her leg wound, in hopes of nurturing tissue growth and keeping infection at bay.

With that completed, the surgeons addressed Nicole's arm. The fact was, on each occasion the medical team had gone back in to look at her arm they saw more tissue dying off, rotting away. They now concluded that amputation was inevitable.

"I think both Nicole and I knew it may not be possible to save all of her fingers," says Hasumie. "At that point, it was questionable. But when she learned about her arm, about how it would have to be amputated, she was so calm. The other nurses were, 'Wow, she's so strong!' If it was me, I don't know how I'd deal with it, but she … whatever motivation she had, it worked for her because she was very strong, you know, on her blog every night, responding to emails. Leading up to the amputation, I didn't see any change in her from the first day."

"I remember one time she actually cried because it was so painful," says Jay Clavio. "And when they decided there was no option other than to amputate, Nicole had this sense of calm. Losing the arm was really the best decision because no one wants to go through life with constant pain. If she was panicky at all, it didn't show. It was an accepting demeanour that she had: 'This is my injury. I have to get better.' She never once thought about the doctors' decisions, never wallowed in her injuries. There was never a time where Nicole was beat up. And on a personal level, I just felt a sense of relief for her. Still, it was devastating because she's a mother and this means a total change of life which in itself is pretty hard. It's huge. It's traumatizing, actually."

With that decision made, and with her leg in a bulky, complicated dressing, she was told to rest.

"Resting isn't exactly easy when they've got a leg vacuum sucking away on you," Nicole explains. "It's a complex dressing but basically, they stuff a huge sponge in your wound, place saran wrap over it to create a seal and then they attach a vacuum that just sucks the junk out that's keeping it from healing."

Keep moving forward, Nicole told herself. *This too will pass. Hang on.*

But Nicole was worried about the amputation. How much more anesthetic could she take? What was her body going to do? She was dreading the pain — she always hated Tuesdays because they were surgery days. "Terrible Tuesdays!" If she was being honest with herself, she accepted her arm's fate. She'd already been told there was too much nerve damage and if they could save her arm at all it would just be a paperweight. "You can keep it attached," they told her, "but you'll have no function and you'll have to be careful you don't hurt it, cut it, burn it, infect it, and run into issues, because you'll have no feeling at all." Still, she was experiencing some slight movement in her hand so she wasn't quite there yet. Until they told her, "The necrotic tissue is getting too far advanced. We need to get ahead of it. Now!"

It was a disappointing end to the fight to save her limb. Still, Nicole felt like it was more distressing to her husband than to herself. That night they discussed how they would tell the girls. The challenge was to find a way to break news like this to young kids without traumatizing them further. Their decision was for Jay to bring Tia and Ella to the hospital for dinner the next evening.

The staff got Nicole looking pretty, and with the help of a ceiling lift placed her into a wheelchair, which she had nicknamed her "hotrod." When the girls arrived for dinner and saw Nicole in the wheelchair, they proudly helped wheel her to the cafeteria. It was the first time since she had left for her Mexican vacation that the girls had seen their mother out of a hospital bed.

"At dinner, I gently explained to my daughters that Mommy's arm was too badly broken and couldn't be fixed so the doctors would have to take it off. Jay and I braced ourselves. We were anticipating a total meltdown. But all we got was Tia being a little pensive, as if processing what that means, and Ella putting her little hand on mine and asking 'Mommy, does it hurt?' Taken aback by her sincere question, the mother in me hesitated, wondering if honesty was really the best answer at that moment. I answered with a truthful 'Yes' and she said, 'Then that's fine. Now, what's for dinner?' That was that. And off they went running around the cafeteria as if it were a huge playground. Kids are so wise, wonderful, and resilient. They took it really well and have ever since."

As usual, nothing was straightforward. One day a tall, indifferent woman strode unannounced into Nicole's hospital room and started talking about how the amputation would proceed and how she could fit Nicole in to her operation schedule in a couple of days. Nicole was shocked. No one had informed her that this surgery would definitely be happening, or that it was to happen so soon. She sensed a holier-than-thou, somewhat apathetic attitude from this doctor, and it was definitely the wrong vibe. "If you're about to entrust your life to someone who's going to hack off your arm, you at least want to feel some measure of good about it," she says. So after the doctor made her exit, Nicole asked the staff who the go-to guy was for orthopedic work. The answer: Dr. John Murnaghan, a surgeon at Sunnybrook's Holland Orthopaedic and Arthritic Centre. Nicole selected Dr. Murnaghan to execute the amputation.

"Once we'd decided on our surgeon," Nicole says softly, "I remember going with Dad to the ortho clinic for the first time, where we discussed amputating. They said it would likely be an above-elbow amputation, which I wasn't very happy about. The more you can amputate below a joint, the better off you'll be, the more mobility you'll have later on, the better time you'll have adjusting to a prosthesis. Dr. Snell took time from her busy schedule — she didn't have to be there — just to plead my case with the orthopedic surgeon, to push for cutting below the elbow. But he wouldn't budge. And I had to accept that John Murnaghan knew what was best."

Meanwhile, in an effort to deal more fully with the wound on Nicole's leg, Dr. Snell had conferred with her burn-surgery colleagues about what to do. They recommended an innovative material called Integra™ Flowable Wound Matrix, "an advanced wound-care matrix comprised of granulated cross-linked bovine tendon collagen and glycosaminogly-can" that's used on difficult-to-treat and unusually shaped wounds. The material is inserted using a flexible syringe, and provides something like a scaffold for capillaries and new cells to grow on.* The surgeons thought it could be a good solution to the problem of how to heal the wound on Nicole's leg. So on March 1, the decision was made to try this innovative approach. With a few more small surgeries and at least a couple of weeks of watching, it was hopeful this process would be successful.

But Nicole woke up screaming.

"Absolutely the worst suffering I have ever felt!" she remembers. "I'd had to deal with a lot of pain up to that point, but nothing as severe as this. It didn't matter what they did to me — and trust me, this poor pain team was doing whatever they could! But something was pressing on a bunch of nerves in my leg and this was the worst electrical pain that anyone could ever endure. It was unbelievably bad. And they were giving me everything they could think of, including ketamine, a horse tranquilizer! That's when I just had a real wake up call for pain. I was beside myself, aching, gripping, and looking at Jay and saying, 'I can't handle this!' I was out of my mind. Jay was beside himself too, watching me suffer with the sickening realization that I was already on such high levels of narcotics but still my pain could not be controlled."

It didn't help matters that Nicole realized her arm amputation was coming up in just days. How would *that* pain be controlled if she was struggling so much now?

---

*Taken from Integra website: www.integralife.com.

The staff agonized, unsure how to react. Up to this point, she'd never complained. But now that she was crying out they knew how bad it must be.

"You know, I still say her ability to deal with pain was unique," comments Dr. Fagan. "Her injuries were horrific. There was so much pain throughout the whole thing. She is one of the toughest women I've ever met in my whole life. She was unbelievable. She muscled her way through it … just grin and bear it. Skin grafting … taking dressings down … it was all excruciating, but she went through it. She actually reminded me of when I played competitive rugby, and you meet some tough guys when you're in that sport. Nicole reminded me of those tough guys that don't even acknowledge pain. Just kind of, 'It's going to happen and I'm going to deal with it, so just go on.' She had that kind of attitude. Amazing."

Eventually her pain subsided. But the high levels of narcotics almost reduced her to a vegetative state. "I remember just nodding off in the middle of things like talking, typing, drinking my milk and spilling it on myself," Nicole says. "I hated the lack of control, being mindless. So I asked them to reduce the meds right away. And you know, we ended up working with the fantastic pain team to find the right combination of drugs to keep me somewhat comfortable, but still able to remain awake enough so I wasn't just drooling uncontrollably while people visited."

Throughout most of this ordeal, Nicole was put on a process of really strict bed rest. She could only rise up with a lift. After several weeks in bed, she was itching to merely dangle her feet over the side. She pushed the staff to accommodate her wish. Finally, reluctantly, they gave in.

Employing great effort and tremendous willpower, Nicole slowly and gingerly touched the ground with her foot. It was a small gain with a huge personal impact.

"I remember putting my foot on the ground for the first time in soooo long," she recalls. "I experienced a bit of apprehension. With the damage to my leg and missing those muscles, what's going to happen when I try to use it? Will it give out? Will it hurt? But when I managed to do it, the feeling was absolutely amazing. I was scared. Yet I was so excited to be able to do that."

Nicole being Nicole — so used to pushing the boundaries — she looked at her physical therapist Bonnie and asked if she could try to stand. Bonnie and Jay just shook their heads and encouraged her not to push it too much the first time. They told her she'd get dizzy. But she persevered. Jay looked on in fear as his wife turned completely white. She was exerting herself so extensively, sweating, clammy. It was terribly uncomfortable for her. This was the first time the blood had flown to her feet in what seemed like forever. *Keep moving forward.*

"Everyone was saying, 'Are you okay?'" Nicole remembers. "And I'm like, 'Yeah, I'm good, let's keep going, let's see if I can take a step.' And I took a step for the first time since that dreaded day on the beach. There are some photos somewhere and I'm just grinning from ear to ear. Something was finally going right and I had control over it. That was sensational!"

But then she collapsed into the wheelchair, spent.

As for the upcoming operation to remove most of her left arm, Nicole confessed that her past nursing experience may have actually worked against her. She'd seen amputations before and felt they were pretty disgusting surgeries. Now it was going to be *her* flesh and bones being sawed into and hacked off. What was it going to feel like after the fact? How was she going to do things? Yes, she was losing a limb, but what else would she be losing in terms of her ability to deal with life? Freedom? What vitality would remain on the other side of this operation? Could she handle the disappointment that was sure to follow? She was apprehensive. Still, she acknowledged the arm needed to come off.

"I remember being afraid," Nicole admits. "The pain team came in and talked to me about pain management and talked about doing a nerve block, which is like an epidural, numbing my shoulder and arm so I couldn't feel anything."

On March 4, Nicole Moore's arm was amputated. The surgery went well.

"I think she actually got stronger after that," says Jay Clavio. "It's really bizarre. Whatever situation puts Nicole at her weakest is where she finds the most strength. I've seen a lot of people break with much less severe injuries, way less severe than what Nicole had. But she's such a strong woman she just kept going. It was always, 'Okay, what do we do next?'"

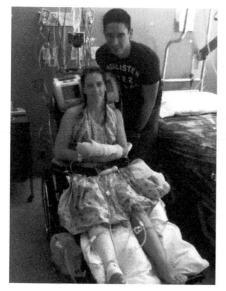

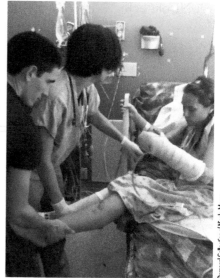

Nicole gets back on her feet.

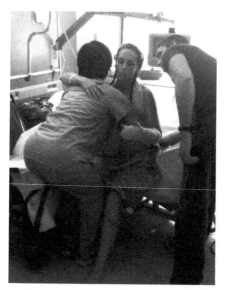

"Here's one of those things I'll never forget," recalls Hasumie. "I had to change the intravenous dressing around the line that was going directly into her heart. And because I was new, I wasn't able to deal with it very often, so Nicole's telling me I'm missing a step as I change the bandage. And I said, 'I'm not quite sure what you're wanting me to do, can you show me?' And then she just started to cry.

"'I *would* show you if I had an arm,' she said through her tears.

"It was just so traumatic. That was the only time I saw her cry. And obviously it was related to her being freshly amputated. She'd come to the realization that she'd lost a limb and for her not to be able to show me how to do the procedure was a serious frustration. It was just so sad. But she didn't linger on it. It was more of a momentary thing."

Nicole kept pushing herself. Long before anticipated or even advised, she began tenuously walking, albeit with a crutch, despite the physiotherapists telling her to slow down. Soon she was regularly able to go to the bathroom or have a shower — the things we all take for granted. What a joy!

Before long, Nicole was also pushing to go home. She really missed her kids. She worried about the strain this ongoing ordeal was taking on her husband and father, who were operating their own Welcome Wagon, regularly bringing her care packages of homemade dishes like lamb chops, risotto, and cakes from a local bakery. She had wasted away to nothing from illness and being bedridden. Normally a healthy one hundred thirty-five pounds, she was down to ninety-eight. As she exclaimed at the time, "I haven't seen ninety-eight pounds since I was eleven!"

Laura reasoned that Nicole heading home would be a real boost for her. They could always worry about creating a sound surgical plan for her leg later. The patient's mental health needed to be considered. Still, Dr. Snell knew this was only a temporary measure. She would eventually want to use a skin flap from Nicole's stomach to cover the bite site and more importantly her femur. "I told her, 'I need you to get fat,'" smiles Laura. 'Just eat, eat, eat so I can get enough skin from your belly.' Then I turned to her husband and said, 'No comments about your heavy wife! I need her fat!'"

Having been told it could be months before she'd be strong enough to leave the hospital, Nicole's determination had finally led her to hear the words she'd waited for: "You are discharged." She was elated. After all the mountains she had faced and conquered, the final summit had been achieved and she could see the peaceful valley of her new life ahead. She made plans to head back to her house in Orangeville. But "Home? No — not yet," exclaimed Dr. Snell, effectively slamming on Nicole's breaks and sending her into another barrier. "You need rehabilitation first."

On March 25 Nicole Moore was discharged from Sunnybrook and transferred to St. John's Rehab Hospital, also in Toronto, a facility dedicated for specialized rehabilitation.

Andrew Fagan recalls Nicole making her exit from Sunnybrook. "You know, it was the last day of my rotation, my last day there. And I watched her actually stand up and walk down the hallway out of the hospital, albeit with a crutch. You look at that and you just say, 'Oh my God, if she can do that, what else can you possibly *not* deal with yourself?' In the end, I drew strength from my experience with Nicole. You don't go through something like that and not walk away from it a better person.

"Nicole's one impressive woman, that's for sure!"

12

Restoring Nicole:
Trials, Tests, and Tasks

St. John's Rehab was unfamiliar territory. Nicole had only been told that this facility was in the business of rebuilding viability following complex, life-changing illnesses and injuries. "That'd be me!" Nicole smiles.

Her immediate reaction to the facility was "It's old! I felt like I passed through some wormhole and ended up in the forties. But the gardens were gorgeous, even in 'sprinter' (my trusty description of the period between spring and winter)."

She was surprised to find nuns from the neighbouring convent walking the halls, ready to talk to anyone who needed an ear, which was just about everyone there.

Nicole also discovered that if she spent ten minutes in the lounge, she'd hear about five different horrific accidents and several debates about whose injuries were worse, and why. Seemed like happy hour at the old-age home, with echoes of residents comparing aches and illnesses. She felt out of place.

Her arrival at St. John's had been a little less than rosy. She desperately wanted to get home and had hoped to leave Sunnybrook and return to her happy life in Orangeville. But those who knew better — her medical team — had prescribed this one last stop.

At first she was at odds with the place, and hardly endeared herself to the St. John's staff, her first question being, "What do I have to do to get out of here?" They told her she'd need at least two weeks of rehab. In true Nicole fashion, she would push those boundaries too. She was out in six days.

Early in her stay she met Dr. Morris Tushinski, who took one look at her and said, "You look stoned." He told her in no uncertain terms that her eyes were glassy and she was on too many medications. He declared that he would stop two of the dosages immediately and decrease the prescription for phantom pain (sensations an individual may experience relating to a limb that is no longer physically part of the body).

Nicole fought back. Her trusted team at Sunnybrook had created her drug regimen and she was not about to forfeit their expertise and extensive knowledge of her particular situation. But Tushinski did not listen. It was his way or the highway.

This created a scenario where Nicole discovered drug withdrawal. "It was unexpected, unbelievable."

She started feeling so nauseous, had so many cold sweats, that she panicked, fearing her infection was coming back. She could barely wheel herself anywhere, she felt so ill. She thought back to her nursing days, remembering how her drug- and alcohol-addicted patients had come into the hospital irate, agitated, and vomiting — a terrible feeling. Suddenly she knew intimately how a junkie in withdrawal faced life.

Calling a nurse, she explained how she was feeling. They quickly administered short-acting pills that would hold her over — like having a quick fix — until her long-acting meds kicked back in.

This was her first day at St. John's.

Still, she was sleeping in a real bed on a comfortable mattress. She enjoyed the nights with no nurses or lab techs coming in to wake her. Gradually she accepted that this was a good stepping stone, to relax and build strength before she went home. She still missed the staff at Sunnybrook, with whom she had bonded so closely, but there was much more freedom at St. John's. And it was peaceful. Ken Mihan even dropped by with his dog and they were able to enjoy some time in the garden, the first opportunity she'd had for that kind of thing in a long while.

At the outset, Nicole did not receive a lot of physiotherapy: the staff first directed her to rest and grow stronger. Part of this stage was working with her prosthetic team. "The best part was getting plastered," she smiles. "No, not drinking, I mean with actual plaster. My upper body was first wrapped in pantyhose, then wrapped in saran wrap. After that, plaster was slathered on what remained of my left upper arm, rubbed, formed, and smoothed until it formed a hard cast. This cast of my stump would be used to make a mould for the beginning stages of a prosthetic development."

Nicole received a welcome break in her regimen when she met another upper-arm amputee named Kelly, who generously gave up her time to pass along tips about prostheses, gadgets to help with tasks, need-to-know tricks, and how being an amputee might be a little easier than anticipated. Kelly left Nicole with an even greater sense of hope and inspiration, for which she felt eternally grateful.

As much as Nicole just wanted to be at home, with her daughters snuggling next to her, she was able to invigorate herself with memories of the good things that had come out of her stay at Sunnybrook. One was a day after her amputation surgery, in early March, when friends dropped by out of the blue with a present they felt could provide lasting comfort while offering reassurance and good cheer.

Cyndi Cramer came up with the idea of a personalized quilt for Nicole. She's a pretty quiet lady; when something bad happens she likes to cuddle into her own self. She wondered if Nicole might like that too. A quilt seemed ideal. And having personalized blurbs on there to say something nice to their cherished friend was a perfect way to get everyone involved.

Cyndi collected thoughts from each of seventeen participants, some of whom had been on the Mexican trip while others simply wanted to express their encouragement. She and Toni picked out the material and then Cyndi started sewing each quote into the quilt. A "quote quilt." In a way it was a means for Cyndi to bond with the girls, but when she was sewing it she could mourn in her own fashion as well.

Here are the inscriptions:

Never underestimate the power of women — Sandra

Keep looking up! — Donna H.

My precious child, it was then that I carried you — Brenda M.

We are family — Toni

New Day, New Beginning — Brenda S.

From caring comes courage, and you cared — Marie

You're an inspiration to me — Ken

Friends are the family that we choose — Terri

Friends are a circle of strength and love — Sandy

May sunny thoughts surround you always — Kathy

A hug is worth a thousand words — Michelle

Turn your face to the sun and the shadows will fall behind you
    — Shari

My thoughts are with you — Donna Z.

Once you choose hope, anything is possible — Tammy

Our friend — Nicole

Love you, Chica — Cyndi

You truly are one in a million in more ways than one! — Janet

When the ladies showed up and presented her with the gift, Nicole broke down in tears. She had always had issues with feeling loved and accepted, sometimes even questioning if anyone really did love her or accept her for who she is. With her mother having left when Nicole was so young, and other setbacks such as having to give up dancing, life had been painful. She was vulnerable, unsure of who or what to trust. But now she realized the true friends she had. Very simply, the quilt changed her outlook on life.

"To say I was blown away is an understatement," Nicole comments. "I couldn't believe all the trouble everyone had gone to for me. And the expressions on all those messages ... wow ... I can't even find words.... Each of these friends has such qualities and strengths, and they all have huge hearts … they make up the best group of friends anyone could ask for. I am a lucky woman to have these wonderfully caring and genuine people in my life."

And the admiration, respect, and love for Nicole Moore goes beyond the Comfort Quilt (which occupies a proud position in her living room today). Comments on her blog reveal so much. Take a look at just a few of the hundreds:

> Nothing, it seems, is going to pull you or kick you down. Your strength and determination are the stuff that most people only read about but you, you are our real-life living example of STRENGTH and a modern day HEROINE.

> You are an amazing woman. With everything you've gone through, you keep such an optimistic outlook on life. You are truly an inspiration to us all. Keep doing what you're doing girl.

> I think of you every day and hope things continue to go well with your recovery. You are an absolutely incredible person, who always holds her head high and thinks of the positive. I wish I had half your strength … you are an inspiration!

> You are a strong lady … I don't know too many people that could endure what you are going through … your operations sound very painful.

> Once again, your words have inspired me to be a more thankful, considerate person. Your tenacity and strength wow me.

> You are so incredibly brave! To possess the courage to fight as you have, to not only survive that horrific shark attack, but to overcome almost insurmountable medical complications, and finally land on your own two feet … is truly inspirational!

> You have been a great inspiration in my life. You are one of the reasons I keep going. I have felt like giving up so many times but

when I read your blog it makes me feel so foolish for the way I am. It makes me come back to earth & realize that my problems are very small. You are a strong and truly wonderful woman.

You are truly an inspiration. Life is fragile and can change in the blink of an eye ... even with no visible danger in sight. I have realized that the people who have experienced the most adversity in life are the ones who love life the most. You find the silver lining in each day ... no matter how difficult a time you are going through. Anytime I start complaining about some trivial matter in my life, my thoughts go to you. You are courageous and uplifting!

Even though the arrival of the quilt was a happy moment, it was also tinged with sadness. One of the women was shocked at Nicole's appearance: she simply could not stand to see her friend without her arm. She walked out. This was Nicole's first realization that her body might bother others, even those close to her.

Though St. John's was another unanticipated stop along the road to recovery, her time there helped prepare Nicole to return home and resume taking care of her children. For this to happen there were certain physical goals Nicole needed to achieve, such as being able to walk with a cane and climb stairs (a challenge when most of your leg's muscle mass is missing). She was determined to keep working at these actions until she got it right. And she was equally intent on making Easter cookies with the girls.

On April 1, after only six days at St. John's — sixty days after the shark attack — Nicole was sent home, albeit with a hole in her leg, her femur exposed to a high risk of infection, and a painful left-arm stump (the reasons for the lingering pain were still anyone's guess). She was ordered to eat well and put on weight. Nursing care and constant dressing changes would see her through this time, but it wouldn't be easy. She'd have to be careful to avoid the kids kicking her or even touching her leg when snuggling, for fear of halting the tissue-granulation process.

Needing relief from the trauma of the previous two months, Nicole and her husband decided to hoodwink their kids. It was April Fools'

Day, after all. Without telling Tia and Ella that Mommy was returning, Jay had brought his wife home while they were at school.

When the girls arrived at the house that afternoon he told them he had a surprise for them and sent them off to search for it. They looked up, down, and sideways, responding to clues given by their dad. But they came up with nothing.

"April Fools," Jay called out.

They responded, "Oh man, we thought you got us the Nintendo we wanted!"

Somewhat irritated, the girls headed to the kitchen, where they finally discovered that Mommy was home. "Words will never describe the outpouring of emotion," Nicole says. "It was one of the most precious moments of my life."

And the Easter cookies? "Best ever," Nicole boasts with a broad smile.

Meanwhile, her father's sister Flori arrived to stay with the family for a while. Her presence was a blessing. Although she lives in Italy, distance never stopped her from being like a mother to Nicole. Flori had been

Mommy's home! Tia and Ella, happy to be with their mom.

there to help with the birth of her niece's daughters, and upon learning of the shark attack had dropped everything and hopped the first flight to North America to act as a surrogate mother (as she had done so often in the past).

"My father and my aunt … I can't even find the words," says Nicole. "It was huge for me to have them there, both physically and mentally. They are both such a part of my life. I would be lost without them. They helped set my mind at ease, especially when facing the uncertainty of the future could be so … so worrisome."

Since Nicole had been sent home to enjoy an all-you-can-eat diet in order to put on weight, Alberto and Flori cooked up a storm. "Eating well in the Moore/Baldassari home is easy," Nicole says, laughing. "It was a good Christmas not having to worry about the waistline that year."

For ten months Nicole did her best to grow her belly. In February 2012 she went back to Sunnybrook, where Dr. Snell took a small piece of Nicole's abdominal muscle and added it to her bite site to help fill some of the void. Next, a large flap of tissue and skin, measuring approximately thirty by fifteen centimetres, was removed from Nicole's stomach and applied to her leg. Thinking about it makes Nicole smile. "In essence, I got a tummy tuck. I joke that there has to be some kind of perk to all of these operations, but it was really strange too. You see, they cut around my belly button to remove the flap, so now there is a mark on my leg where my belly button used to be. I'm my own version of a patchwork quilt." But the piece the surgeons removed from her stomach was so large that when they went to close her they realized it was a little too snug. Nicole couldn't lie down flat for weeks.

"Despite my best efforts to pig out, I had only grown enough of a flap to cover the exposed femur," she explains. "While that was crucial, the back of my leg couldn't be covered by the flap. It would have to remain covered only by a skin graft. And that meant a future surgery."

Once again, there was no easy solution. Nicole's determination would be tried anew as the healing process failed again. She ended up contracting a threatening infection under the flap, against her bone, hindering the healing. The medical team mentioned osteomyelitis, which Nicole knew all too well often leads to amputation. Dr. Snell had to go back in yet again and debride the tissue back down to heal.

This time it seemed to work; no osteomyelitis. As for amputating Nicole's leg, for the time being they seemed to have dodged that bullet.

But for how long?

Forever?

It was too soon to answer that question.

13

Sharks: Gotta Love 'Em

Amazingly, sharks are seen by Cancún's diligent hotel staff members nearly every day, but they often lack the communications processes or systems to provide adequate warning. Or they may not want to disturb the guests, who might be motivated to seek alternate, less dangerous, destinations in the future.

Dwelling in the shallow waters of Cancún's beaches, bull sharks are more dangerous to humans than any other species of shark. People are not first on its preferred menu, but some attacks are the result of territorial disputes. Bulls are extremely territorial, and will immediately attack animals that enter their space.

Just prior to Nicole's life-altering attack, the hurricane that washed out many of Cancún's beaches has altered the habitat where sharks congregate, leaving them somewhat disoriented and defensive. That kind of behaviour had made the sharks even more dangerous.

Despite all this, you may be surprised to learn that bull sharks are an extremely threatened species. They are being killed faster than they can breed. Many are yanked from the water by fisheries workers, who hack off the fins for sale to affluent Asian customers seeking to sup on a specific, well-known soup. Often trolling illegally in "protected" waters, the workers will throw the stripped shark back into the sea still alive, where it will bleed and be unable to swim. The sharks then die of suffocation. This happens to approximately forty million sharks annually.

It's hard to feel compassion for sharks, despite how rarely they pose a danger to humans and how greatly humans imperil them. Still, they capture the human imagination. Great works of literature are peppered with references to sharks, from Hemingway's Santiago to Verne's Nemo

Jose Angel Astor

Jose Angel Astor

to Melville's Ahab. More recently, Jacques Cousteau's fascination with sharks has captivated many an imagination, as does Juliet Eilperin, national environment reporter for the *Washington Post*, who writes about pursuing sharks and the people who love and hate them.

After writing *Jaws*, Peter Benchley discovered that sharks are quite different from his fictional barbarian. "I couldn't possibly write the same story today," he stated in *Shark Trouble*. "I know now that the mythic monster I created was largely a fiction."

Our impressions are driven by terrifying movies and memorable descriptions by people like Captain William E. Young in his 1934 memoir *Shark! Shark!*

> The very word summons up a powerful mental image of a cold-blooded rover of the deep, its huge mouth filled with razor-sharp teeth, swimming ceaselessly night and day in search of anything that might fall into the cavernous maw and stay the gnawing hunger which drives the rapacious fish relentlessly on his way. There is something particularly sinister in a shark's appearance. The sight of his ugly triangular fin lazily cutting zigzags in the surface of the sea, and then submerging to become a hidden menace, suggests a malevolent spirit. His ogling chinless face, his scimitar-like mouth with its rows of gleaming teeth, the relentless and savage fury with which he attacks, the rage of his thrashing when caught....

Read that and then try feeling warm and kindly about sharks. But after reading this chapter you may just change your mind.

Sherman's Lagoon, a long-standing nationally syndicated comic strip, stands out as a humorous look at the beast of the sea.

"I probably should have picked something with a friendly image to focus on, like a dolphin or a seal, not a shark," says Jim Toomey, creator of the comic strip featured in over 250 newspapers in more than thirty countries around the world. "Then I'd be relaxing on a yacht in the Bahamas! But I had developed a fascination with sharks as a kid. The

Jim Toomey.

Jacques Cousteau documentaries really turned me on. The shark had always been depicted as the bad boy but Cousteau changed all that. So a shark it was when I initiated *Sherman's Lagoon* in 1991."

One thing this amusing comic strip does is reduce the mystique. "The shark is a complicated character," Jim explains, "a little like Frankenstein — a misunderstood monster. Sharks are a lot more than 'a mindless eating machine' as they are described in *Jaws*. So I decided to make my lead character a great white shark. I set out to make sharks a little more complicated than folks figured. And, you know, many people have changed their opinions of mice because of Disney. Sure, it's a little more of an uphill battle with sharks, but I wanted to bring out real ocean facts. After all, Sherman is a very talented animal: he can smell a drop of blood a mile away, he can sense electromagnetic vibrations ... so I hope to use the comic strip to educate people a bit about the reality of sharks.

"Mind you," Jim adds wryly, "I was originally thinking more along the lines of an underwater Snoopy. I had visions of ShermanLand in Tampa, Florida ... but it didn't work out that way. Another reason I'm not on that yacht in the Bahamas!"

Not everyone has been a fan of this scheme to humanize sharks. "Sure, some people expressed the opinion, 'The fewer sharks the world has, the better,'" Jim says. "You know, 'Why do we care about an animal that doesn't bring anything of value to the planet?' It's an ignorant point of view, but it's out there. Luckily not in large numbers."

Still, Jim recognizes that not everyone shares his views. "You know, if I consider Nicole Moore, or Bethany Hamilton the surfer girl, or the family of Adam Strange who was killed recently by a shark, what do you say to them? I'm in a very awkward place in that conversation. Obviously if you lose a close family member, it's a real, tangible problem, not an abstract conservation issue. But we can't make nature safe for everyone."

He cites an example to support his point. "Public safety and ecological value are two different issues. What if there was a beautiful, pristine river — say in Montana — and a canoe tips over and three people drown. Does that make the ecological value of that river any less? No. It's similar with sharks: they are very occasionally responsible for the deaths of people or, in Nicole's case, serious injury. But does that make their ecological value any less? No. There's no connection between public safety and ecological value."

Jim knows whereof he speaks. Beyond making a living as a cartoonist, he has a master's of environmental management from the Nicholas School of the Environment and Earth Sciences at Duke University. He's on the board of directors of Mission Blue — the Sylvia Earle Alliance, a network of nonprofits organized to create marine sanctuaries. "Sylvia wants to change the world with 'hope spots,'" he explains. "Our mission is to create marine sanctuaries in eighteen places in the oceans. Right now, only 1 percent of the ocean is fully protected nationally and internationally. We need to change that, not just to save sharks, but to save the world."

Jim is also working to abolish the odious practice of finning. "It goes back centuries," he says. "It wasn't a common thing until thirty or forty years ago. It's primarily a Chinese custom, serving shark-fin soup at a special banquet, a display of wealth. But it's a very wasteful practice. The commercial fishing outfits catch sharks, cut off their fins, and then discard the whole shark. You see, the fins are where the money is. It's less than 5 percent of the shark, but shark-fin soup sells in restaurants for $160 a bowl. So you fill your boat with fins, not sharks."

The irony is that apparently shark-fin soup doesn't even taste that great. In fact, many restaurants — up to 40 percent — have been found to be selling a fake soup featuring no shark fin at all.

The cartoon that Jim drew for Nicole's birthday.

"I get emails from people in Asia who are sympathetic to what I'm trying to do." Jim explains. "They say, 'I think shark-fin soup is disgusting.' But they are in the minority. In the U.S. and Canada, pressure is creating change. But not in China. You have to get the government to end it there."

Jim suggests a key to unlocking the Chinese mindset that values shark-fin soup: get young people onside. "Make it uncool with the younger set in China," he says. "They are a lot more open to environmental arguments than the older generation who are the ones buying the soup."

And there's some good news. Wild Aid (www.wildaid.org) reports the demand for shark fins is finally in decline.

Jim Toomey has a special talent that enables him to respect sharks and appreciate the lighter side. You can learn more about the work Jim and his associates are doing at www.mission-blue.org.

In honour of Nicole's birthday, Jim sent her a special drawing.

Jim's suggestion of getting youth involved to curtail finning fits well with the work of Claudia Li, a Chinese Canadian who emigrated from Hong Kong to Vancouver with her parents. "Just by coincidence, a friend of mine asked if I'd seen a film called *Sharkwater* by Canadian producer Rob Stewart," she explains. "I got a copy, sat down to watch, and was mesmerized. I knew then I would never be the same."

The award-winning *Sharkwater* documentary debunks the myths about "bloodthirsty, man-eating monsters," and explores the exploitation and corruption of illegal shark poaching.

"I watched *Sharkwater* alone and couldn't get over it," Claudia remembers. "It was so profound. It convinced me that I had a mission: to find a way to reach members of my own Asian community and get them to abandon their ritualistic obsession with shark-fin soup at important gatherings."

This would be easier said than done. "People didn't even think about it," she explains. "I mean, it was just, 'Hey, you're getting married, gotta have shark-fin soup.' Just like having turkey at Christmas … you just *do* it without asking why."

Claudia set about establishing Shark Truth (sharktruth.com). Her immediate goal was to change customs. Enlisting family and friends, she invested $700 to build a website promoting a bottom-up and top-down approach to make change.

When asked if she worried about the former generation's reaction, she acknowledges the potential for backlash. "The last thing I wanted was for my folks to feel I was unappreciative about the efforts they'd devoted so my generation could excel. I made sure they realized I was grateful. But just as they had done things to create change in my generation, so too I wanted to promote change in theirs."

What got Shark Truth off and running was Claudia's creation of the "Happy Hearts Love Sharks" Wedding Contest. The campaign engages with consumers and businesses, encouraging them to go fin free. Her "Make a Vow to Go Fin Free at Your Wedding" appeal recognizes that for Asian families the marriage celebration is the time when shark-fin soup is most often served.

"When you and your partner decide to keep sharks in our seas instead of in your soup bowls you'll have a chance to win a once-in-a-lifetime honeymoon trip to the world-famous Galapagos Islands for a six-day deluxe cruise," the contest promo explains. "All you have to do is submit a photo and story about yourselves … the couple with the most votes will win the grand-prize honeymoon trip."

The program has taken off, attracting youths who can, in turn, influence their parents and older generations. "So far, we've diverted eighty thousand bowls of shark-fin soup and saved eight thousand sharks," Claudia says proudly.

But her work goes beyond promotions for weddings. "We need to support legislation that protects sharks by stopping the import, sale, possession, and trade of shark fins. Shark Truth encourages political leaders and activists to engage and consult with all stakeholders involved before introducing legislation."

One of the more fascinating individuals in shark research interviewed for this book was Dr. Eugenie Clark, senior research scientist and founding director of the Mote Marine Laboratory in Sarasota, Florida. Dr. Clark's work has been covered in magazine and newspaper profiles and several books and textbooks. Sadly, she passed away in February 2015, at the age of ninety-three.

"Most people fear sharks because they do not know them," she said. "That, or they have been influenced by media and books, especially

Jaws. But once people learn about and understand sharks, their perception often changes to one of respect and awe. After witnessing the fear instilled by his book, Benchley became an advocate for sharks and wished he had not written such a successful story."

This was a woman who put her aqualung where her mouth was. Genie spent boatloads of time beneath the surface of the world's oceans, swimming with sharks. "No creature on earth has a worse and perhaps less deserved reputation," she explained. "I have found them to be normally unaggressive and even timid toward man. The vast majority of them are 'chinless cowards': unless provoked or threatened, they prefer to retreat rather than challenge anything as large as man."

Her curiosity about fish and their behaviour was a driving factor in Genie's work since she was nine and saw a shark for the first time at the New York Aquarium. Because the water was murky, she'd press her face against the glass and pretend she was walking on the bottom with the

Dr. Eugenie Clark.

fish. She decided then and there she wanted to study the ocean, but her mother suggested taking up typing so she could assist researchers. That didn't sit well with the spirited young lady, who shunned the maternal advice and set out to study living sharks in 1956, when she realized there was a lot more to learn about these amazing creatures.

During her long career, Genie witnessed many positive developments and was grateful that so many people and organizations have come to recognize the importance of sharks and their significance in maintaining the balance of the ocean ecosystem. "The tide is changing, and people are realizing the great exaggeration of their danger. In fact, you are in more peril *driving* to the ocean than you are *swimming* in it.

"There is so much fear mongering within our culture. It's not fair, but at least it's going in the right direction. People are now recognizing sharks are not the mindless eating machines they were once perceived to be. And now it's the shark that needs to be protected from people."

Meanwhile, discussing Nicole's experience, George Burgess from the Florida Program for Shark Research and International Shark Attack File explains, "The fact that Nicole was washing sand off her body — creating disorder in the sequence of the sea — may have suggested to the bull shark that this was a fish in peril, which would be a food opportunity. Then came the bump-and-bite routine. Eventually, the shark decided she was not the best morsel around and left."

Eugenie Clark's take: "When we are in the ocean, we need to be aware that we are in the shark's habitat. I agree with George Burgess completely and would add that Nicole washing the sand off her body may have created vibrations in the water similar to a struggling fish. Although it is rare for a shark to come back and bite a human more than once, there are a number of documented cases where they attack again. I myself reviewed a shark attack that occurred in 1958 where a small boy was in the shallows and was bitten three times by a tiger shark."

Eugenie Clark was one of the many proponents of shark protection, recognizing that if they disappear from our oceans there will probably be a lot of rotting coral reefs. She was also a great supporter of extending research in order to better understand these intriguing animals.

"The more you study a creature, the more understanding you can gain. The shark is certainly the most spectacular story to follow."

14

"And Now, the News..."

In the age of smartphones, Facebook, and Twitter nothing newsworthy stays quiet for long. Nicole Moore's shark attack was receiving international headlines in the blink of an eye.

"It went global right away, pictures and everything," says Carlos Da Silva in Cancún. "I was getting calls to the hotel literally from all over the world."

"I get it," Nicole says, with more than a hint of frustration in her tone. "Who doesn't want to hear the gory details about a girl getting attacked by a shark?" She understands the human propensity for rubbernecking. We want to see, yet we don't want to see.

The media assault on Nicole Moore and her family and friends was overwhelming. *Everyone* seemed to feel it was their right to get the details. Nicole appreciated that the incident was international news, but she was unprepared for the intensity of the intrusion into her life. The media clamour became so incredibly invasive, so stressful, that it surely did nothing to aid her recovery.

Industrious reporters tracked her down at Hospiten Cancún and began badgering her for interviews. Not what you need when you're sick, tired, and in pain. According to some Mexican reports the attack was her fault: she'd apparently been feeding the sharks, they'd suddenly turned on her, and she'd lost an arm and a leg as a result of her foolishness. They even got her name wrong, identifying her as "Nicole Ross." She was frustrated to say the least.

Nicole finally decided to throw in the towel and grant an interview to one reporter while she languished in the Mexican hospital, purely to set the record straight. "I'll give you an exclusive," she told him, "but damn it, get it right! Stop the rumours, because people back home are freaking out."

Things were even worse when she returned to Canada. Nicole just wasn't ready for the tenacity and persistence of the hungry journalists. Eventually she found herself yelling into the phone, "Leave me alone! Leave me and my family alone! I'm not ready for this. How dare you do this? Don't you have any heart?"

"Yeah, but it's a great story," was the usual callous rejoinder. "Just spend a bit of time with me to answer my questions. It won't take too long."

"I became really pissed off at them," Nicole says. "I ended up just refusing to talk to them all, period. Nobody."

Sunnybrook's PR representatives came to the rescue, offering to field calls. They put out media releases to calm the ill-mannered masses. Even so, there was the occasional reporter walking into Nicole's room unannounced, searching for a story. She was horrified at this assault on her privacy. And when she learned her children had been approached by a journalist on the driveway of their Orangeville home, and that her neighbours had been pestered too, she lost it. It was just too much for her to handle.

How could they involve children like that? She was fighting for her life in the hospital, and now she had to worry about her kids too. Frustration and angst were high. Nicole had no idea what her daughters were hearing. She was anxious that Tia and Ella were being exposed to false information and it might freak them out.

Even the hospital was ready to give in. The PR lady finally approached Nicole and suggested doing a media scrum in a controlled environment in one of Sunnybrook's boardrooms. There'd be a back door for Nicole to enter and leave from whenever she wanted, so she could avoid being bombarded. The hospital rep reasoned that if they gave the press what they were after perhaps they'd realize "story over" and retreat.

Nicole didn't want to do it at all. What was she going to say? Would she go in a bed? A wheelchair? Would she be lucid through the array of drugs she was on? But she gradually came to realize this might put an end to the cacophony and agreed to try.

It only partially worked. The media still wanted more and more.

Nicole had an idea. Jay's best friend is Rusty Thomson, a radio show host at Windsor's 89X-FM. The two grew up together in Parry Sound. Nicole reached out to Rusty for advice. She explained the situation and the decision she had come to: offering one more — and *only* one more — interview as a tactic to keep the hounds at bay. But which media outlet should get the nod?

Rusty agreed with Nicole's strategy and recommended CTV, Canada's largest private television broadcaster with the number-one national newscast.

Reporter Michelle Dubé rose to the challenge and conducted a respectful interrogation. Dubé is known for telling people's stories accurately and has interviewed celebrities like Oprah Winfrey. Nicole felt comfortable with her. At last, Nicole felt her story had been told faithfully. Could she now just get back to focusing on survival?

The swarm of journalists were somewhat satiated, but there still remained the legion of friends, family members, and interested parties who were deluging Nicole with emails and Facebook messages.

Her good friend Maureen Van Damme had a plan to help with that.

"My husband Dan is a techie guy," Maureen explains, "and early in Nicole's Sunnybrook stay we talked about setting up a blog for her … it would reduce the pressure on her to communicate and she could post and receive comments at her pace, only when she wanted to."

Nicole Moore's Blog, mooretolife.ca, became an overnight hit with those who cared. And there were many.

"It was cathartic for the first two weeks," Nicole recalls.

But then it too took on a life of its own. The blog became a lot of work because, in true Nicole fashion, she wanted to respond to everybody. And she wanted to do it with excellence. She even wanted to approve all entries before they got posted, a very time-consuming daily exercise. Between this and being full of drugs and pain, her days were difficult at best. Not to mention having only one hand to type and dealing with her dyslexia. Add in visitors and it was more work than she'd counted on. "Even for me to do a small blog entry, I'd be writing for two hours trying to deal with the affect of those drugs and falling asleep on my keyboard."

Still, the blog was worth it. She had only to look at all the people who were writing to her and carrying her when the going got too tough to manage on her own. It meant so much.

After Nicole returned home and set to work on her strenuous rehab routine, she felt compelled to return to the scene of the crime.

"It's hard to explain," she says. "When something this awful impacts your whole life, you just need to go back and touch it, feel it, taste it. You just can't let it go, you know, relegate it to your past. You need to meet it head on, now, when you're in control, on *your* terms. And so I really wanted to go back there to that beach in Mexico, thank the hotel folks who had been so helpful, the ambulance driver, the guys on the beach ... just to make peace with the whole situation. It was an important part of healing."

In fact, Nicole was bound and determined to face her fear head on: head to the beach at the Grand Park Royal Cancún Caribe hotel and walk out into the Caribbean Sea exactly where the bull shark had assaulted her life. She would master the influence that had become the ruler of her existence.

She also planned to meet with the personnel at Hospiten Cancún and demand the medical records that were rightfully hers — documents that could finally put to rest the growing doubt about the treatment she had received while under their care.

Nicole had contacted Ken Mihan to see if he might be able to arrange a freebie flight through Air Canada. He managed to come up with a buddy pass, the kind Jay had used to get to Mexico. Ken had some downtime coming up so he was prepared to accompany her on the trip. Carlos Da Silva came up with free accommodation at the Grand Park, so all the details were falling into place. But as much as Nicole wanted to make this excursion, she was still full of butterflies. Having Ken with her would be comforting.

Just before leaving for Mexico a producer for *The Fifth Estate*, a CBC TV program, contacted Nicole to request an interview. She declined, explaining that she was heading to Cancún. Intrigued, he felt this could be a great story and asked if their crew could accompany her. "No way!" she answered.

Known for their determination to go beyond everyday news into original journalism, the producers of *The Fifth Estate* had the audacity to announce that, despite her objection, a journalist and crew would meet her at the airport. To say Nicole was shocked and taken aback would be putting it mildly. She felt sick to her stomach. The trip was already stressful enough. This was pushing her emotional limits. She didn't need the added hassle of dealing with reporters and possibly unravelling on camera. Wouldn't they love *that*.

Unfortunately, there was nothing she could do other than set the ground rules. At the airport, when she first met the producer and crew, she made it clear that she was not impressed. "You'll have to do it my way or no way at all," she informed them sternly.

In Mexico she eventually relented, giving them the interview they so desperately sought. She even allowed them to follow her to the beach, where she explained on camera what had occurred. But through a combination of emotion stemming from recalling the event itself, and anger bubbling up from under the surface due to these media invaders, she came close to tears.

Despite their presence on the beach, Nicole was able to master her fear and walk into the ocean in the spot where she was attacked.

"An experience like a shark attack doesn't really recede from your mind," she concludes. "But faced with the stress of trying to survive and making really key decisions about my health and trying to stay positive and not worry about my kids ... what with all that, the memory of the media invasion is the one I'd love to throw into the trash bin.

"It was a truly traumatic time, especially when more trauma was the last strain I needed."

15

The Lunnie Bin

It's a cold day in mid-March, cooler than predicted, and there's a hint of snow in the forecast. The girls are off to school, Jay has knocked back breakfast and is off to work, Alberto is busy checking news feeds on the computer.

Nicole grabs her lined parka, slips her right arm in, and whips it around her body with a quick twist, catching the coat as it comes about so she can pull it across herself — a one-arm move she's perfected with practice. Satisfied that she is protected from Old Man Winter, she beckons Marley the puppy. "C'mon, buddy, you need to pee."

Marley is quickly obedient and they return inside. Nicole, shivering from the frosty temperature, pats the dog and says, "Good boy. Let's get some breakfast." She pulls the can of dog food from the fridge and opens the pantry door to get the dry stuff. Getting around the kitchen used to be so easy, something she could do in her sleep. But with the lack of an arm and hand, and the need for balance alertness, it's not quite as simple as it once was. Still, practice makes perfect and she gets the job done.

"See you later, Marley," Nicole calls out as she enters the garage. The big SUV with license "F1 MOM" (a gift from Jay, a joke about his wife's lead foot) awaits her. How she used to love jumping into anything on wheels and gunning the engine. These days, though, she finds herself being a bit more circumspect.

Climbing up into the driver's seat, she reaches across her body and bends her right hand down to grasp the seat belt. Pulling it across herself, she lifts it up to her mouth, where she clamps down tightly on the fabric with her teeth, holding it in place while she manoeuvres her arm more to the right. ("If my dentist knew I was doing this, he'd have a fit," she muses. "Actually, now that it's in this book, I guess it's out there. Busted!") Grabbing the seatbelt again with her right hand, she pulls it down and locks the device into position. "Good to go."

Fifteen minutes later she arrives at the Eramosa Physiotherapy Associates building. The exterior sign promises "Excellence. An evidence-based approach to physiotherapy."

"Hey, Nicole, how are ya today?" The receptionist greets her like an old friend. In fact, they are chummy, because of Nicole's many, many visits to this clinic and their kids hanging out together.

"Brent ready for me?" Nicole asks.

"You bet. Go right in."

Nicole moves through the spacious facility with the assurance of one who has travelled these halls numerous times. She arrives at a suite and immediately lies down on the therapy bed.

For the next hour, she and registered physiotherapist Brent Lunnie will try to fix her broken body. "It's my weekly trip. 'Going to the Lunnie bin.'" She smiles.

But what she experiences over the next sixty minutes is no laughing matter.

"In the beginning, I had to travel for more than an hour to a physiotherapist," she explains. "Had to find someone to drive me — I was immobilized in a brace — paying for all that gas ... we're talking about several times a week. Really inconvenient and very painful having to get in and out of the vehicle all those times. But finally I was able to connect with Brent, who's right here in town. Not only that, he's so good and knowledgeable at his job."

Brent has worked in the trade for over ten years. A partner in the clinic, he is proud of the up-to-date, research-supported physiotherapy strategies he uses to help clients understand their treatment, while providing a professional environment to remedy their concerns in a realistic timeframe.

"Same old, same old today, Brent? Or something new?" Nicole asks about the procedures she will experience.

"More of the same, Nicole," he replies. "We'll warm up your muscles, ligaments, and tendons, we'll stretch them and use effleurage massage to get the circulation going. Then ultrasound and, of course, acupuncture to help with the pain."

"Ahhh, yes," she grimaces, "help with the pain. That would be good."

Much of the physio involves "mobs": techniques to encourage mobilization. Brent works with her arm to increase the range of motion, the goal being to ensure it doesn't freeze up or develop shoulder atrophy.

The injuries to Nicole's leg have resulted in loss of all of the capillaries and veins that are meant to return the circulation, resulting in circulatory problems. Brent massages her leg and gets her doing active and passive range-of-motion exercises.

"When I first came in here I was pretty braced and could barely move my leg at all, couldn't lift it. Now I'm walking, full range of motion on my knee. I came in with crutches, but now I even walk without a limp. Lot of goals accomplished."

Referring to her amputated left limb, Nicole tells Brent, "I seem to be experiencing a higher degree of pain." This is an exacerbated level of suffering, since each and every day Nicole's arm will present a sharp, almost electrical stabbing sensation that is an intermittent ache, like she's sticking her finger into a light socket. When it takes hold of her she catches her breath, then eventually it fades.

"Okay," Brent says, "I'll see what I can do to lessen that."

The two of them work together, tag-team physio. It's been that way for almost two years. Nicole's nursing knowledge and natural curiosity fuel her understanding of the procedures being applied, which supports Brent as he works to maximize the strategies he's developed.

"When I try to use my quad muscles, like when I extend my leg, my brain and nerve pathways just don't realize that most of those muscles are gone," she explains, wincing with pain. "So it's like I'm trying to use absent muscles. It pulls on the massive amount of scar tissue, and this causes my leg to cramp and hurt. But it's not unbearable ... it's much better now."

After the previous "Plan B" operation in 2012, Nicole could not even lift her foot off the table. It was dead and numb. As much as her brain was telling her leg to move, the signal wasn't getting through. There were certain movements she simply couldn't accomplish. "It felt so odd, especially with the numbness, like an epidural that only worked on certain parts of my leg." She smiles. "One doctor stated that this was likely due to a nicked nerve during the last surgery. But finally, after several months ... the nerve seems to have repaired itself. I can move my leg. I'm hopeful that it will be the same with the nerves in my stump."

"Needless to say, I had never dealt with the victim of a shark attack," Brent comments. "The only thing that would be even close to the degree of trauma Nicole has experienced is serious motor vehicle accident sufferers or an Afghanistan war vet I'm working with, who has major wounds. But none of that compares to Nicole's situation."

Brent recalls his initial assessment when they first met: "Her injuries were really significant, certainly nothing that I'd ever seen before collectively. I've treated amputees. I've treated people with soft-tissue injuries. But collectively, nothing like this. So I had to research how we could best address this situation. Some of it was back to basics: there was limited range of motion and we needed to get that back. Keep muscles loose and prevent things from tightening up. Then we could work on strengthening afterwards. Pain management for arm aches and nerve throbbing. I also knew there were more surgeries pending so it was a matter of improving things as much as I could prior to her re-entering the hospital. So the preliminary goal was to get things moving and build up strength. Right now we're just trying to maintain the goals Nicole has achieved and address any situations that have come up."

The main problem with Nicole's recovery has not been her leg, it's the arm. "My arm pain is not normal," she explains. "Like most amputees, I have what's called 'phantom pain.' I look at my stump, see that my arm isn't there, and my brain seems to register that understanding ... yet when I'm not looking at my stump and doing other things, my brain makes me feel like my arm is still there. Unfortunately, my brain only remembers the traumatic arm, mangled and twisted in a contorted state with my hand flexed up close to my heart. This twisted imaginary limb that my brain won't let go of incites a pain response, and that causes me to feel the ache of the injury every day."

Phantom pain typically lasts for a year or two. It's been over two years for Nicole, but she's hopeful that the part of her brain that holds memories will soon accept the loss of her arm, just as her common sense has. "Phantom pain is the normal part. But of course *I* can't be normal. I have to outdo everyone." She laughs. "I experience an intense electric pain, like sticking a finger in a light socket, with any touch, pressure or vibration to my stump. That includes walking, driving, or hugging. This is what prevents me from wearing my prosthetic. If I wear it for more than ten minutes it causes incredible, long-lasting pain. An MRI showed a tear to one of my tricep nerves and my orthopod thinks I may have torn this nerve and possibly others during the battle I had with the shark. The only choice I have is exploratory surgery, which may make the nerve injury worse. It's that, or wait and see. I'll think I'll just wait and see if it will back down on its own. It is tolerable. Far better that it was two years ago."

In the meantime, acupuncture, ultrasound, transcutaneous electrical nerve stimulation (TENS device), physio, and meditation help with the pain. A strong constitution and meds help too.

In the hospital, when Nicole was enduring so many surgeries, she recalls being administered serious doses of narcotics. "I was on such high levels of pain meds that I'd often hear my health-care team say they'd never seen anyone taking that much narcotic and still be awake and talking. I'm not sure that was a good thing," she adds with a laugh. She was able to get off most of the narcotics quickly, but was discharged home on a strong dosage of Hydromorph Contin, a highly addictive drug that she didn't want to be taking for long. Unfortunately, due to risk of shock to the body or withdrawal, meds of this kind can't be stopped abruptly.

"I was able to get off that three months quicker than they said I'd be able to. I'm not too anxious to get back on."

Today she is only on Gabapentin, typically used for the treatment of seizures and neuropathic pain. Most amputees are on this medication, and it will be a lifetime med for Nicole.

Meanwhile, Brent is inserting acupuncture needles. "At first, I do feel pain as the needles stimulate the nerves," she says. "But then it warms and subsides. It's funny, I leave here feeling worse. But then it feels better later. And if I miss it, even if I'm off by two to three days, my pain levels just start creeping up and it takes a while to get 'em back down.

"But I do look forward to coming here. Yes, I know it will hurt but I'll be better for it."

The former personal trainer pauses for a moment and looks a little sheepish. "I also need to get back to the gym and strengthen myself more," she confesses.

"Nicole is the benchmark," Brent sums up. "She is — even comparing her to my MVAs or my Afghanistan vet — she's overcome far more than any of them have in their recovery. We've had one little cry in two years, one day. No pity party. She is the top. It's mind over matter, strength of character, Nicole's desire to excel … it's all of that.

"But of course, she's aggressive and impatient, so she tells me we have to look at bigger goals, like getting her back to skiing or snowboarding, get back to working.

"She's amazing."

16

Life Interrupted: The New Normal

The Greek philosopher Heraclitus wrote, "Change is the only constant." Nicole and her family now know this to be true. Their lives have been completely transformed by a single incident that occurred thousands of miles away and lasted mere seconds. It's truly amazing how such a swift event can assault every aspect of a family's existence.

"I'm a logical person, ducks-in-a-row sort," says Alberto Baldassari about the suspension of his family's day-to-day activities. "So this offends my natural sense. Sometimes I get tired of remembering things about this horrific time. I just don't want to think about that anymore: enough is enough!" He is upset that more than two years after the shark attack in Mexico the incident still impacts the daily hustle and bustle of his family.

"Am I changed? Yes! The image of my daughter in the water, on the beach ... it still sticks in my mind. It keeps coming back, gives me a little bit of agony there when I think about it. It's just an ugly picture. And it won't go away. Not so much a nightmare as anguish...."

"I'd say the shark attack dominates who she is ... who *we* are," adds Jay. "I mean, Nic's personality hasn't changed ... and she's still a beautiful woman ... but more than two years later, you just can't forget such a thing."

Jay's a private man who's not really comfortable with being "the shark lady's husband." Talking about it peeves him. He'd prefer separating his life from this as much as possible. He's introverted, not a public speaker. Nicole is okay with doing presentations, but not him. "She can have it."

He is frustrated by how much the shark attack still affects every aspect of their lives. "It's still pretty fresh. I understand ... but it's so much not who Nicole is. I mean, she's always a happy person, always smiling. Who she is now is exactly who she was then. But what's changed is that she's been attacked by a shark. So that dominates us all of a sudden. She's 'the shark lady,' like it or not. That's how it is, not positive or negative, just how it is. My reality is that people always ask how my wife is doing. Sure, I appreciate their interest but ... well, there's more to our lives than sharks, you know."

Each member of the family has had to adjust to Nicole's newly defined abilities. They have their good days and bad days. Jay is task-oriented: if the house is dirty, he'll clean it. If this or that needs doing, he's on the case. The problem is that he ends up stepping on Nicole's contributions to the household, without meaning to. He accepts that she can't do all the things she used to, but for him to do everything makes her feel useless. Jay admits he forgets about such things sometimes, and needs to be reminded that there are two people involved. He also understands that her personality and his don't always mesh at times like that. "But at the end of the day, I love my wife for who she is. Sure, she's not physically the same person as she once was, obviously. That's just the reality of our lives, I can't change that."

At that Nicole grins. "Jay's right. I'll admit it: I'm a bit of a control freak. So when he starts over-achieving with keeping the house going, I feel like I'm not keeping up my end. But I also feel like I'm losing authority in running things. You know what: if that's the worst thing that could happen out of this, it's more than manageable."

Still, underneath her cheerful exterior, Nicole worries that the new normal is not fair to her husband.

"This is not what he signed on for. I'm no longer the beautiful girl he married. Physically, I'm maimed, I'm marred. He's a good man and he would never turn away. I think he is the best man in the world, no one else tops him. And so I think he deserves better, he doesn't deserve this."

Jay scoffs at that. "Nic is a beautiful woman. Not just to look at, but her spirit ... I mean, how lucky can a guy get?"

Still, sometimes when she feels she doesn't look the part, it makes her feel really bad for him. The strong side of her acknowledges that there is deeper love there and she's a good person, and there's more to the two of them than this situation. But there are days where she just has to go along with assimilating the adjustment. All part of moving forward. Yet as much as moving forward, sideways or backwards can symbolize progress, practical matters still present challenges.

"Getting dressed is absolutely the hardest part of my day," Nicole explains, showing a bit of unease. "Putting on a bra is easy: I just don't undo the clasp. I pull it over my head. But putting on clothes, hands down, it's the most frustrating thing.

"As soon as I wake up, as soon as I sit up, I get pain. There's nothing I can do about that, but there's a sharp, shooting pain and I have to catch my breath. It's my first reminder. *Good morning!* My second reminder is, okay, I need to get dressed. It really is very difficult. Coats are tough: too many layers. Once I realize I can't wear this or that, the problem is the time it takes. I want to get things done but, 'Oh yeah, I have to slow down.' Well, I don't like having reins on me. I'm a move-forward person. Now I have to move slowly, differently. It's frustrating, life-changing ..."

Bathing is another challenge. A simple thing that you do every day: jump in the shower. You don't even think twice about it, right? But try taking off your clothes when you have one arm and one hand. Try stepping up over a four-inch ridge into the shower when you lack muscles in your left leg and can't bend it. Try showering when you have to confront balance issues that make you a little wonky on your feet. How do you shampoo with one hand? How do you apply soap to your arm or shave your underarm?

It's those little things you take for granted. Like taking a coffee out to the car and then confronting how to open the door. Like wanting to apply moisturizer to your right hand. How the hell do you do those things?

And what about intimacy? "It's the biggest monkey on my back," Nicole explains. "I can deal with other people staring at me, I can deal with the therapy, the pain ... but crawling into bed at night with my husband, I always, always feel, 'Oh, I need to hide that side.' Why does my husband have to go through this? It's one more reminder that my life isn't normal. I hate to burden people and definitely don't want to weigh down those I love."

After surviving such an ordeal, Nicole's attitude at first was "I don't care about my scars and who sees them." She had hoped to continue wearing bathing suits and sleeveless shirts. But she quickly learned that as much as she was okay with that, others were not.

"Some folks are a little squeamish about looking at my stump or the wound on my leg. I've actually lost two close friends because they said it was too difficult to see me with one arm. 'You're different now and you have to accept that people will react this way,' one of them told me. It hurt deeply and despite my 'I don't care about scars' attitude, my 'I don't like making people uncomfortable' trait is stronger. So I've had to accept that my appearance and how I dress might bother somebody. I wear a cover up with a bathing suit and I think twice before wearing a spaghetti-strap top outside. I still wear them, but I think twice."

She can deal with people looking at her, but what bothers Nicole is that now, when people do look her way, they see the amputation, not the person. "It used to be that people would come right up to me, look me in the eye, and connect with me … but now they first look at my stump and become uncomfortable. I see it. Even if I'm okay with it, others are not. And that makes me *not* okay with it."

She's also had to accept she'll never have any feeling in her left thigh. If a dog jumps up, she won't feel it. She needs to be careful that she doesn't cut the delicate skin. She can't go up or down inclines very well, because the shark bite left her without half the muscles normally needed just for walking.

Buying clothes, a formerly pleasurable pastime, has lost its joy. This became evident when Nicole decided the time had come to head to the mall, take her time, and find something nice to wear. But after a trying afternoon she was forced to resign herself to the fact that clothes now fit her differently.

"There are only certain things I can wear that don't show," she says with a bit of remorse. "And then others, I can't get into or out of them…. On that first day I went shopping, I actually left bawling. I am not a crier. I don't cry. But on that day it just all seemed to come home. Suddenly it was no longer a joy to shop. I can't even wear jeans."

But in characteristic Nicole Moore style, the melancholy is quickly replaced by buoyancy. "Now I shop for my kids. There's my out! I love it."

Many amputees carry on their lives with the aid of a prosthetic device. But this is another bad card dealt to Nicole: she still can't use the prosthesis provided for her due to the severe pain it brings. A reality she accepts — for now.

"I remember the happy day I got my prosthetic," she says as her face lights up. "It was like Christmas for me. I had been working with my awesome prosthetic team at the SCIL lab at Sunnybrook for over a year to find the right fit. I opted for a mechanical prosthesis — one that works on my muscle movements only, no electrical components. I could work it really well, but everything we tried caused so much pain to my stump. They couldn't figure out why it hurt, but they never gave up on me. I'm sure it was frustrating as much for them as it was for me. I wanted it so bad."

When they finally discovered the reason for the pain was the torn nerve, not the prosthetic itself, the final apparatus could be completed and Nicole was able to take it home. But it just sits there taunting her. "Maybe one day I'll actually be able to use it," she says wistfully.

Despite all that, there is good news. Nicole doesn't have post-traumatic stress disorder. "I'm very lucky. I've never had nightmares, flashbacks, or panic attacks. No trauma. I really don't know why I haven't suffered like so many others have, but I'd say that talking and blogging about the whole ordeal and my feelings while in the hospital … well, it kind of got it out of my system. And I received such a tremendous amount of support. I also believe that I did the best I could throughout this. Even though so much was out of my control, I handled the things I could."

She pauses reflectively and looks around, a peaceful smile appearing on her face. "It's also because I'm just so grateful and happy to be alive."

Her extraordinary ability to focus on the positive side of life is an amazing advantage.

"It's hard for my mom getting around the house and stuff," says Ella softly. "I couldn't do it. Tia and I are more helpful because Mom only has one arm, so we make our beds and have to hold the toast for her to butter it … and we set the table. I feel sorry for her because it's hard having one hand and not two."

"She's a strong person because she survived that whole thing," adds Tia. "She's special: she was attacked by a shark, she's recovered … it just feels normal now. I don't think about it."

Tia pauses to reflect, then adds in obvious admiration, "I couldn't have gone through it."

A glorious spring morning is dawning on the outskirts of Orangeville. The newfound warmth of the sun blends with the aroma of an unfolding season. It is the fifth day in a row that the temperature has climbed above zero, following a drawn-out winter. Birds wing overhead, returning from the sultry south, while flowers and buds dare to reveal themselves to the uncertain conditions. Before long the bikes will be wheeled out of the garage and the grass will need cutting. Golf will be in full swing.

But Nicole is sitting indoors, in the living room of the lovely house she designed. Soft classical music plays in the background, something by Tchaikovsky that she finds motivational and soothing. It is peaceful.

The home was built in 2006. The floor plan is open, spacious, with high ceilings, soft-coloured walls, and dark wood floors. It's elegant, yet not over the top, reflecting a busy family on the go.

"I'm certainly not an architect but I did have a great time working on design ideas with the builder," says Nicole. "And we ended up with a pretty neat home in a fabulous neighbourhood. We're all very happy here."

The topic soon switches to the spirit of hope under duress that sets Nicole apart.

"People say to me, 'I could never do what you did!' But you never know what you're capable of. Not until you're actually faced with it. We are built to survive. It's in us. You never know how strong you are until being strong is the only option. You are braver and smarter than you think. You can get through anything!

"One moment should not define you. It should only strengthen you. Don't give up. Don't quit. Just say, 'I can do that!'"

Nicole admits that if she was not endowed with that kind of positive philosophy things would be different.

"If I didn't have that spirit, I would be totally lost. I'd likely be saying, 'I don't know if I can get though this, I'll never be the same, I'm ugly' and I'd probably fall into a depression. I would not have fought as hard. I would not be where I am today. It would be too easy to just sit down and do nothing and feel sorry for myself and not heal my wounds and not stay on top of things and just give up on life. You know, 'Oh the pain and oh I can't get up and oh poor me …' But after a while you need to have the attitude of 'chin up!' What else are you going to do? You can only stay down for so long."

Sports help keep her grounded. In 2012 Nicole participated in the Warrior Dash, a gruelling mud run that demands tremendous physical prowess — the kind of courage and feistiness that few people with two arms and full leg mobility have. "I did it simply to prove to myself that I could. It was symbolic to me that obstacles aren't going to stand in my way."

There was one problem: Nicole had just completed the "Plan B" flap surgery to cover her left femur, and it had yet to heal. An infection was preventing closure. Dr. Snell tried multiple procedures to help it heal, but nothing worked. "Laura called me to her clinic two days before the

Personal Collection of Nicole Moore

Nicole (in the centre) at the 2012 Warrior Dash.

Dash," Nicole says. "She opened up and debrided the area then sutured it extra well in hopes that the wound wouldn't tear open. Then her nurse Leslie and I came up with a waterproof dressing to block the mud and water. All of this so I could do the Dash because they knew how important it was to me. Talk about patient-centred care! It might seem trivial to some, but when you are forced to face obstacles in your life and then are given the opportunity to grab them by the horns, to actually do it is really liberating."

"Turns out a little mud bath is exactly what the doctor ordered. The wound finally healed after the Warrior battle."

Nicole completed the whole Warrior Dash and has done so every year since. She is a warrior! And for 2015 she's extended her journey even further. "I made myself a shark-bait shirt with a new logo: 'Bite Back,'" she explains with a proud smile. "I also decided that for 2015's Warrior Dash I would wear short shorts that bare my scars for the first time. I'd never done this before in public, but I wanted to show my commitment to keep on fighting and never be ashamed!"

Indeed, Nicole triumphed and completed the course like never before. "Definitely sore and bruised up," she texted, "but man, I rocked that Dash today! I accomplished obstacles by myself that I've never been able to do without help before. It was an amazing day for me. The announcer at the event saw my shirt and questioned me a bit about the attack. When I told him that I've been doing the Dash every year since the shark attack, because I won't let obstacles stop me, he was a bit speechless, then said, 'Wow … I love that attitude.' It was great!"

When people say, "My life is so terrible," Nicole is the first one to tell them to keep on going. She knows that her life could be far worse, and that there's always someone worse off. She feels that if people facing adversity can just keep moving forward they can learn from their past and forge ahead with positivity. She's used her motto, Keep Moving Forward, forever.

"There's something good that's come from this, something that's actually changed me," Alberto comments. "I always thought she was good, a good kid, always very proud of her. But I never thought she had this kind of strength … never in my life. It one hundred percent floored me. What I see her going through … people don't understand, to go through all of these months of agony, pain every day, tissue rejection, constantly for months … that's what makes the story compelling: a human being that finds some incredible strength at a moment where I believe I would have given up."

"Nicole is such a positive inspiration for everybody," says Sandra, one of Nicole's exercise-class friends. "It doesn't come across what bad fortune she's had. If you don't know the details, as we do, you'd never get an idea what this poor girl has been through. Even simple things like making dinner, getting dressed … it's unbelievable what she has to endure."

Nicole at the 2015 Warrior Dash.

"She makes you realize your problems aren't a very big deal," adds Kathy. "I don't honestly know how I'd handle the challenges she's faced. She's so strong-willed. I don't think she's even had a nightmare about it. Not sure that would be me."

"Nicole is a special lady," says Ken Mihan. "I've never met such a positive, fun-loving lady in my life. It doesn't matter how much she gets kicked in the head, she finds a way to bounce back and make something positive out of it … such a positive attitude. Most people would be down in the dumps. But Nicole? She's got her kids, she's got her husband, she's got her life: to her everything's good, she'll make the best of it. She's inspirational."

Yet, even the most optimistic beings among us have to deal with reality from time to time. And the irrepressible Nicole Moore has her moments.

In 2013 Nicole returned to work at Headwaters Hospital. "Obviously things had changed for me and I wasn't able to go back to acute-care nursing. So we had to see where I fit in and what positions were available." She is currently part of the leadership team as a hospital supervisor. It's an integral role at the hospital, with significant responsibility.

"I confess I've had to really focus on the positive aspects of this new job," Nicole says. "Frankly, it's not a job I'd ever seen myself doing but opportunities present themselves for a reason. There's been a huge learning curve and a shift from clinician to managing, and I'm still striving for my footings. The fact that the team believes in my ability to fill this role says a lot to me. But I sorely miss nursing. It lies in my heart. What I'm doing now is not the hands-on nursing I both love and get gratification from. Giving it up, even temporarily, is heartbreaking for me. It was my calling. I'm still mourning the loss of it."

But her grieving won't stop her from taking this opportunity and doing the best job she is able to. "I can still make a difference to the staff and the whole patient experience. And that's a good thing. Yet, you know what: life's too short … if I can't find true satisfaction in my career, then I have to accept it's time for a change."

What becomes clear now is how the power of positive thinking contributes to Nicole's life in a way that can be summed up in one word: happiness.

"No question, I'm happy. Happiness is a feeling. If you really feel deeply satisfied with who you are, I think you're a happy person. Some people want money or material things. For me, I wake up, sure I've got pain, but I'm healthy, my kids and my family are healthy, we have a roof over our heads, we have love. To me these are the basic essentials: if you are loved and you can love, that's what completes you. What more could I ask for?"

Does it seem hard to believe you're reading the words of a woman who was nearly killed and had her life changed forever?

"I'm not hard-wired to be happy," she says. "I had to train myself to be that way. I felt gloomy when I was younger. But I turned it around. And today I have a positive disposition no matter how dire the situation gets. I wouldn't say one hundred percent, but pretty much. Where it's not always positive and upbeat, I always think our life is still fine. It would take an awful lot to destroy my positive outlook."

Of course, her confidence isn't bulletproof. She admits that personal relationships play a big part in how she feels. She deeply values what her dad feels about her, same with her husband and kids. And if a relationship is strained, it plays on her. If she punishes the girls, she feels bad. She's an emotional person, so if she hears about someone else being hurt, especially a kid, that brings her down. But she seems to balance it well.

Still, she hates to be a burden to anyone. Should a sad occasion occur or when she deals with harsh pain (still a regular event in her life), she keeps it close to her chest. "I don't want to bother people. And that's not necessarily a good thing because I'm pre-deciding what people want to hear. But that's me. If I have an issue, I'll tell you. If you piss me off, I'll let you know. I cry by myself, not in front of others.

"We don't always have control over things in life. You need to just accept that's the way it is. Focus on other strengths when things get you down."

With a warm look appearing on her fetching face, Nicole states matter-of-factly, "It's pretty simple, really: when you give, you feel better about yourself."

17

Keep Moving Forward

The brutality of Nicole Moore's shark attack did not go unnoticed by the Cancún Hotel Association. All the hotel directors got together right away, analyzing the situation with experts in oceanography and ocean life and specialists dedicated to investigating sharks. The authorities agreed that Nicole's attack was very strange, very rare. One explanation put forth was that when Hurricane Wilma hit Cancún in 2005 and washed out the area's waterfront, officials hired a European firm with special machines to rebuild the beaches. In order to do that, they unknowingly took sand from a shark habitat, essentially removing the sharks' natural environment. This left the animals disoriented, wandering around trying to find a place to gather again. Because of this, the experts determined, it wasn't a hunger attack on Nicole, it was a defensive assault. If it had been hunger, Nicole would have been okay. But when a shark is acting defensive and disoriented, look out.

Of course, the men on Jet Skis ramming the shark, trying to get it out to sea, would have contributed to its bewilderment as well.

Out of the hoteliers' meeting evolved several recommendations to hopefully prevent such an occurrence from ever happening again. "We have to accept that we are using the ocean to entertain our guests," explains Carlos Da Silva from his desk at the Grand Park Royal Cancún Caribe. "We are not ocean experts. We are administrators of a hospitality business. Nicole's attack was new to us. We were unprepared. We had already learned the hard way how to prepare for a hurricane, but this was something totally different."

For the Grand Park, the new strategy meant hiring more security staff and placing sentries equipped with binoculars on the roof of the hotel, scanning the ocean from 6:00 a.m. to sunset. If they notice anything suspicious a code is triggered and guests are instructed to get out of the water immediately. Red flags are put up on the beach.

Carlos: "Since the situation with Nicole, we've had that code a couple of times. Were they sharks or just dolphins that the guys saw? They don't know and I don't know. But I never again want to go through what happened to Nicole. So we play it safe and make sure everyone gets out of the water."

The Mexican Coast Guard has manned up as well. Boats now patrol the beach areas and are connected to the hotels via radio. If they spot anything, they let management know right away.

"We're doing a better job, no question," says Carlos. "I'm just so sorry it took what happened to Nicole. She is such an amazing woman. I mean, where does she get the courage to come back to this place? Where does she get the nerve to go back into the ocean at the exact place where the shark attack happened?"

Several miles down the road from the Grand Park Royal Cancún Caribe, Hospiten Cancún, where Nicole was treated, boasts on their corporate website about being part of an organization that is proud to offer the following:

Hospiten Group is an international network of private hospitals, with over 1,000 beds, committed to providing high-level health-care services. We see over 600,000 patients every year. All of our centres are equipped with the latest technological innovations in the medical and management fields, and are staffed by a team of recognized professionals providing the top-level healthcare services that characterise the Hospiten Group.

Alberto Baldassari isn't buying it. "They may be recognized professionals providing top-level healthcare services to *some* people, but not to my daughter. There were too many things occurring there that

I didn't like. Attempting to do what they were not qualified for was a mistake."

Alberto is of the opinion that gross incompetence occurred at Hospiten Cancún. His conversations with a local Mexican lawyer led him to understand that he needs to provide the Canadian medical records to a Mexican litigator. Then a conference call would occur between these two lawyers and Alberto, wherein he would be advised whether there is potential for proceeding legally. "If there is," he explains, "they will subpoena the records from Hospiten — the ones Nicole has tried to get and has had no success in obtaining — if they exist at all. At that point, the litigator would assemble an approach to go before an arbitrator. It is this individual who would decide if there is a case or not."

As an experienced businessman with international exposure, Alberto is approaching this situation with his eyes wide open. It's a little uncomfortable to be dealing with a different system and a different culture. "I'm not being unkind when I say I've heard stories. Is someone on the take? Who knows?" Still, as a practical and logical person, Alberto will deal with this carefully. "I can say this: if it's a long shot and we don't like our chances, we'll forget about it."

Paul Addlestone of JET I.C.U. has an opinion as well. As a medical professional who has seen hospitals around the globe, when told that Hospiten Cancún boasts the highest levels of medical expertise and care his response is vehement: "Yeah, yeah, but haven't you heard about those websites touting a five-star resort with the best restaurants and fabulous beaches … and when you get there, it's an absolute dump. I wouldn't want to have a thorn removed from my foot at any one of those facilities down there in Mexico!"

And Dr. Andrew Fagan, having moved from Sunnybrook Hospital to work in emergency medicine in Calgary, offers this: "I have no doubt Nicole's bandages had not been changed for many days in Mexico. She came back from there with life-threatening infections … that ultimately was our biggest concern when she first arrived because she was bordering on necrotizing fasciitis in her leg: flesh-eating disease. You don't do anything about that, you die in six to ten hours! She was at that point, and that's why we worried we'd have to amputate her leg."

Would Nicole still have her left arm if the Hospiten staff had been equipped to provide a higher level of care? Would the limb be "normal," or with limited function? Would her left leg be better off? Would she have endured less excruciating pain and suffering during the many operations and in her hospital stays, and even today? What other impacts will she experience over the rest of her life that are a direct result of alleged incompetent medical approaches?

This only scrapes the surface of the questions that need to be answered before legal action can go ahead. Counsel will define the lawsuit if the dispute moves forward.

Nicole has assessed the legal question too. In the beginning, her father respected her wishes to hold off on any action. She felt that the Hospiten team had saved her life. As a member of the medical community herself, she could only offer thanks for their care. It seemed a slap in the face to turn around and question their expertise.

Still …

"I would really, really like to know what the Mexican doctors did in the OR," she says. "What did they actually see? Was there so much debris in my wounds that they washed it out as much as they could? I'd like to have some kind of belief, some confirmation, that they were doing the best they could. I'd like to get a feel for what they saw on my arm. That's where I think they are holding back my medical records. How bad was the arm? Did they really feel they could save it? If I knew what they saw, I could compare it to what it looked like when I got to Sunnybrook. And I'd like to know if there was a dressing change? I don't recall one. I know in the last three to four days there wasn't. I would feel better knowing they were doing all they could do. But I'm just not certain … and I don't like feeling that way."

Time has not alleviated many of Nicole's physical challenges. There have been many slowdowns due to losing her left arm, and there is only so much she can learn to do to get around this disadvantage. Pain has continued to be an issue — the stress of her return to work in hospital administration resulted in a recommendation to attend a pain clinic.

Sadly, her recent surgery was not quite the unqualified success she had hoped for. The operation, carried out in the late winter of 2015, was designed to cover the rest of the void on her left leg that had remained shielded by only a few millimeters of skin graft since 2011. The goal: "Better lookin' legs!" she says with a smile.

She went into the surgery excited. After all she's been through, you have to marvel that she could express such elation at the prospect of more doctors, more hospitals, more surgery, more recovery …

"I had six tissue expanders inserted into my legs," she explains with a nurse's keenness for medical procedures. "They kind of look like deflated breast implants. Then, over the next several months, I injected those spacers with saline to slowly inflate them and stretch the tissue in order to expand the epidermis surrounding them, the objective being to create lots of skin for reconstructing." If she were not an experienced nurse, she would have had to go into a hospital to have the stretchers expanded, a small stroke of good fortune that makes Nicole smile.

"After everything was stretched, they took the implants out and used that new, extra tissue to reconstruct my legs. Yes, I said 'legs,' as in plural. The shark, thankfully, only bit one leg but the doctors removed a huge donor flap from my other one to attempt the first flap operation back in 2011 — the one that failed." Her eyes look downward. She's still put off by the unsuccessful procedure to this day. "That donor site had only remained covered by a skin graft for three years," she explains. "Now the vulnerable muscles and nerves are finally covered and properly protected."

But, as with so many aspects of Nicole's many surgical procedures, this one did not go totally as planned. "I'm not sure what happened, and no one's talking, but my right leg — my good one — has circulatory issues and is now numb. No feeling at all. Something occurred in that surgery that has left me with two less than perfect legs. Surely that was not the plan."

Nicole had been hopeful that this operation would be the last of her surgeries. At this point, she's no longer sure of that outcome.

Perhaps it *is* time to consider compensation for her setbacks. Nothing can rewrite history, but if her situation is the result of mistakes, she's beginning to feel that she and her family should benefit from some form of recovery.

"The records that Hospiten appeared to give me during the filming of *The Fifth Estate* piece were not, in fact, the official health records that I was requesting," she says. "Without any records, it's just guessing. And that's not good enough."

18

Inspiration: There's Moore to a Life Resumed

To be in a position to inspire is truly a gift. This feeling is what drives Nicole Moore today. She's finally accepted that.

"If I was made to go through all this for something larger, I figure it's for a reason: to share my story with people who are experiencing setbacks, adversity, suffering ... if they can be motivated by my approach, then I will surely feel that this has been worth it."

She hesitates, considers this last thought, and reconsiders. "Well, maybe not *totally* worth it, but ..."

This book is one way Nicole has chosen to give back. Friends and visitors to her blog had felt her natural inclination toward a positive, optimistic perspective could motivate others to feel the same way. They urged her to put pen to paper. "But I've never thought of myself as someone who inspired others," she says. "The way I see it, I'm just a normal person trying to make my way through life the way we all do. And I never really wanted to write a book about the shark attack that has ended up truly assaulting every part of my life. I'm not the kind of person who's into self-promotion and while that commitment to keep moving forward has always guided how I handle challenging times, it never dawned on me to share my approach with anyone. I'm just me in the same way you're you, no more or no less important."

But Nicole eventually relented and agreed to telling her story in print in the hopes that it could help other people facing what seem like insurmountable odds.

"To those of you considering my story and perhaps staring down challenges of your own that threaten to stop you dead in your tracks, know this: you have the power and strength within you to beat the odds, to survive, and to move on. I did it, and so can you. And if people are able to suffer less while summoning the will to advance forward because of my story, then I'm glad I told my tale."

"My journey toward coping with a new life isn't over. Whether it's discovering how to confront the daily challenges of living with one arm, or learning ways to move about with limited mobility, or dealing with the media, or even surviving the stares I get in public, it's a learning experience. For me and my family. But I've got a lot of living to do. And in many ways, I'm just getting started."

That message is echoed in Nicole's speaking program. Supported by a slide presentation, she tells the audience, "I'm not here to lecture you or to tell you how to live your life … I simply want to share my story with you."

It's an intense, passionate presentation. Audiences are rapt, striving to make sense of what they are hearing, both the experience of the shark attack and then the overwhelming medical challenges that Nicole

Nicole speaking.

has since faced. But what really shines through is Nicole's determined, positive character, focusing on her encouragement to avoid letting life's challenges get you down. "Enjoy the benefits of living a full existence rather than the disadvantages that might hold you back," she advises.

When time permits, Nicole offers to answer questions at the end. "The first thing everyone wants to know is, 'What kind of shark was it?' I guess they want to see if it was like the one from *Jaws*." Too bad it wasn't. That fish was a great white, somewhat of a pussycat compared to the ferocious bull shark."

To say "you can hear a pin drop in the room" is no exaggeration. Former mayor of Orangeville Robert Adams says, "As she spoke, I had tears in my eyes and a lump in my throat. Nicole's motivational speech inspired everyone in attendance with her strength, courage, and determination." An amazing person!

While she's busy inspiring others, she's also being inspired herself. Nicole was blown away by her community's efforts to raise money for her to purchase a prosthetic arm. Even before she had returned from the hospital, the Orangeville police department played hockey against

Personal Collection of Nicole Moore

The baseball fundraiser. Nicole is in the front row, far right.

some National Hockey League alumnae and then handed her $5,000. Another community silent auction raised $17,000. A charity baseball game generated further funds.

"I was floored at the support," she says. "People were coming up to me ... people I didn't even know ... and they're making donations. How do you even begin to acknowledge such kindness?"

What has this whole experience taught Nicole? Laughing, Nicole states, "I learned that whoever invented bedpans was a sadistic son of a bitch! And I learned that hospital food is not really food!"

She pauses to let the whimsy pass, then becomes serious. "I've learned how strong I am. I always thought I was strong-willed, strong-minded, but I surprised myself at just how determined I can be. And I have to say I'm pretty proud of how I've endured. I've also learned who my friends are, which is really gratifying. I've learned how deep my husband's love is for me: to see the pain on his face and emotional breakdown, I've never seen him like that before. But he has coped and tolerated the changes to our lives. I've learned that despite my will, I don't always get my way: I haven't ridden a bike — *yet*. Or skied — *yet*. Or nursed — *yet*. I've learned to be a better mother: I'm more patient, more appreciative. I used to be tired, short tempered. Now I stop myself and make sure the kids are my priority. Let's see ... I've also learned that my one wish would be to undo all of this."

She looks around, like she's hoping someone will tell her it somehow *can* all go away. "Of course, that's not realistic," she acknowledges. "Besides, I still believe things happen for a reason. I'll never know why, but hopefully I can learn to pay it forward. Maybe there's a greater good in all of this."

And in a twist that some people struggle to understand, she has also become an earnest, steadfast supporter of organizations that seek to save endangered sharks. Nicole has survived while they may not and it weighs on her.

"These incredible animals are just being decimated. They are being slaughtered unmercifully just so illegal raiders can hack off their fins and then throw the sharks back into the sea to rot like so much trash. If you haven't done so, you need to see Rob Stewart's film *Sharkwater*. It will bring tears to your eyes, it's so brutal."

Some people think she should want the sharks dead because of what's befallen her. But Nicole just doesn't see it that way. "I happened to be in the wrong place at the wrong time. Let's face it, I was invading their world. That shark was not only disoriented but provoked by the Jet Ski guys … the shark's not the bad guy here. In a different scenario, that shark and I would have shared the beach, just happily swimming along, oblivious to each other."

She stops to reflect on her concern about sharks and her worries about the overall degradation of the world's oceans. "If it's fallen on me to help, then I'm ready!" As Wendy Benchley, *Jaws* author Peter Benchley's widow and noted ocean conservationist, commented recently to *Shark Assault* co-author Peter Jennings: "I am one ripple, you and Nicole are other ripples and, when we combine them with the efforts of thousands of people around the world, I know we will make big waves of change for ocean conservation!"

Being ready to change also means belonging to Shark Attack Survivors for Shark Conservation, a group of people from around the world who have actually survived shark attacks and who have joined the Pew Environment Group's effort to restore and conserve the world's dwindling shark populations. They volunteer their time to educate the public and persuade decision-makers to take action to save sharks.

But it is another group, The Bite Club, that has given Nicole a more defining purpose. Started on Facebook by a small group of Australian shark-attack survivors, they seek to spread the word that shark-attack survivors and their families are not alone. The members take comfort from knowing there are other survivors available to speak to, message, email, or even meet. Dave Pearson, one of the original members, who was attacked in March 2011 while surfing in Australia, has become affectionately known as the gatekeeper of the group. "We have found in our own experiences that we can help each other through the hard times," he says. "We are also willing to share information with all people who are interested in the devastating effect an attack can create and the inspiring stories of survivors who have overcome the adversary of an attack and have become inspirational to those who know them."

The Bite Club has grown to include 240 members, including survivors, family members of survivors and of those who have been lost to shark attacks, friends who have witnessed their mates being attacked, rescuers, and many more. Amazingly, the group has encountered people posing as survivors just to poach stories or to advance their own political agendas. It is developments like this that the legitimate members find hard to cope with.

"One of our first overseas members was Nicole Moore," Dave says. "Her story touches you on so many levels and for her to have such a positive attitude has been such a great personal inspiration of mine. Nicole has every right to be bitter and angry, but her zest for life and the love she has for her family helps her triumph through all the lows that come with the recovery from an attack. Due to the great friend we found in Nicole, we now have international members from Brazil, Florida, New Zealand, South Africa, and Reunion Island, to name a few."

There's one more group Nicole belongs to, an elite assembly of thirty special people: "This is a private enterprise where we can communicate openly without fear of being judged or even ridiculed," she explains. "When you express public views for the world to see, people tend to get passionate and opinions become divisive and heated … you know, like one group wanting to protect the sharks and another figuring they should be culled. It's amazing how folks with their own agenda actually become abusive in their beliefs, and after everything that I and the other thirty members of this group have been through personally, who needs that? So Beyond the Bite has become my 'sharky family' and I chat with them frequently. Their words, feelings, honesty, and vulnerability not only make me feel like I have people who understand this unique shark-attack world that we struggle with in a variety of ways — such as handling post-traumatic stress disorder (something I have managed to avoid but others haven't) — but they also make me feel privileged. It is a tough initiation into an extremely exclusive club, but I feel lucky to have them. Over the last couple of years, I feel that a special bond has been forged, especially with the founder Dave Pearson. My goal is to travel to Australia to meet these wonderful people."

Life is moving on. The blog — once a key tool for Nicole to keep in touch with her flock of friends and strangers who care so deeply and wanted to be in the loop — no longer seems necessary. Life is returning to normal. Or the "new normal," as Jay refers to it.

"Sure, I'm 'the shark lady' to some folks," says Nicole, somewhat wistfully. "And I guess I'm okay with that. But I'm so much more than the shark attack that changed my life. Will the time ever come when I can wake up and not think about it on a given day?"

"Will we ever get over it completely?" Alberto muses. "You do get used to this kind of thing to a certain extent because, let's face it, life must go on. But forget about it? You can't. Life has changed."

At the end of the day, the Moore/Baldassari clan is united in their feeling that it would be pleasant never to have to think about sharks again. But Nicole accepts that's just not in the cards. The pronouncement she makes is so indicative of a gifted survivor who came up against the unthinkable and conquered the forces seeking to end her life.

"I've been given an opportunity to make a difference. Some people — most people — never get that chance. But it's been handed to me and you just can't take that lightly. There's a responsibility there, a duty … I'll never be the same after what's happened. And no one who's close to me will be the same. But that's not all bad."

She stands up. Watching her, you'd never know that inside she is dealing with the pain of that simple action. She checks her watch: time to take her next round of pain meds.

It's been a long day. The girls will be home shortly. Jay in an hour. Alberto is ready to talk about what they'll make for dinner.

Nicole turns her head to gaze out the window. She's lost in thought as the sun begins its gentle arc toward the horizon.

With her most recent operation being less than successful, perhaps the time has not yet arrived where she can finally put the physical healing of this brutal assault behind her. The memories of the other less than successful procedures gnaw at her from time to time. Like the significant pain she endured in her arm after the amputation because of a torn tricep nerve. "No one had taken the time to investigate the area leading up to my shoulder," she explains. "It had frozen and my stump had a torn nerve, likely because of the incredible force the shark had when it pulled on my arm. The neurologist was supposed to repair this but it didn't happen." Her voice fades off. No point being angry now. Too little, too late. But still …

Her mind drifts back, returning momentarily to the grand adventure that has overshadowed her life for more than four years, a journey that has wrenched her broken body and wounded spirit from the greedy hands of death only to triumph in a way that few people could. She has met the test. She has beaten back the odds. She has taken what could have been a tale of loss and turned it into a story of survival.

"I intend to see that the world is not the same again," she says firmly. "It's going to be better. It's going to have people in it who are suffering life-changing setbacks and who, after hearing my story, realize their time isn't up: they can keep moving forward.

"And it's going to include the people who are destroying sharks meeting a fate they deserve."

Nicole smiles to herself. "If I can add my little voice to inspiring that kind of change, then it's all been worth it."

Nicole, Tia, and Ella.

Personal Collection of Nicole Moore

Mooretolife.ca
Nicole's Blog

Beginning in February 2011, Nicole Moore felt a need to communicate with the numerous friends, relatives, and strangers who had become aware of her situation. As she lay in the hospital, countless messages were coming her way. In Nicole's caring manner, she was concerned they were going unacknowledged.

A blog seemed like the most practical way to keep interested parties up to date as well as receive — and comment on — their observations. And so mooretolife.ca was born.

Nicole's blog is recreated here, minus the comments of other contributors, which we have omitted to preserve their privacy.

My Story

Okay … I know everyone wants to know the real story since the media has made a debacle of the entire incident, AKA Nicole Ross. After waking up and hearing about the media reports, I now understand why so many people were freaking out after reading the media's account of how the story unfolded. So here is the general scoop straight from "shark bait's" mouth …

I was away in Cancun with a group of friends. On January 31, I had just finished playing a game of beach volleyball when I went into the water to rinse off. A couple of Sea-Doers off in the distance were yelling at me in Spanish and waving me to shore. I was only waist high in the water so I couldn't understand how I could be in their way or why they were so mad but turned to head into shore anyway. That is when I felt a bump and the shark's teeth sinking into my left leg. As my blood started to turn the water around me red, I knew what had happened the minute it happened. Everyone asks how I felt at that moment and the answer is scared sh*#less but what I thought was that sharks like blood and that I had to get out of the water so I continued heading to shore. Before I knew it, a shark (same or a different one I don't know) bit down on my left arm and it wouldn't let me go. The shark was pulling me so with my right hand I grabbed its nose and pulled my left hand out. The Sea-Doers were close by but unable to grab hold of me, I just kept thinking of my children, and just kept inching toward shore. Eventually one of the Sea-Doers was able to grab my right hand and pulled me up onto the shore. People were buzzing around me, speaking only Spanish, but unfortunately I don't speak Spanish so I laid on the beach feeling completely helpless, aware of injuries and the severity of them. Fortunately, two young nurses identified themselves asking me my name and telling me that they can help. I told them my name and that my leg needed a tourniquet. Selflessly a man applied pressure to my leg while someone else was able to place a tourniquet. I then told the nurse that my arm was bleeding badly and needed a tourniquet too. I believe that swimsuit strings were used to control the bleeding and that this was the single greatest contributor to me reaching the hospital alive. I lost a tremendous amount of blood and because so many people offered help to me, I am here to tell my story and grateful to so many people that I will never even know. Even though I was attacked by a shark I consider myself to be extremely lucky.

Welcome to my blog!!

Posted on February 11, 2011 by Nicole Moore

I have felt an overwhelming amount of love and support since my shark attack & this seems to be the best and easiest media available to communicate with everyone. This page, in fact, is evidence of the support I have received and was made possible by my dear friend Dan Van Damme, whom I thank from the bottom of my heart.

Please note that I believe in respectful communication and privacy. To ensure this I will be reading messages prior to posting to the blog.

I'm looking forward to hearing from you all.

Categories: Uncategorized | 88 Comments

Bad Day

Posted on February 14, 2011 by Nicole Moore

Morning all. Today is a bad day. My leg had developed a complication and they are taking me to the OR shortly. I likely will not be on the blog for the rest of the day so I wanted to apologize if you post something and it does not make it up on the blog today but please keep the comments coming.

I love them. Keep those prayers coming too as I really need them today.

I'll let you all know how I'm doing when I can.

Categories: Uncategorized | 31 Comments

A New Beginning.

Posted on February 15, 2011 by Nicole Moore

Good morning everyone.

Thanks to everyone for your support, concern, love, and prayers yesterday. It was a bad day but it's over and today is a new day.

So what happened yesterday you ask. Last week, the wonderful team of plastic surgeons were able to rebuild my left thigh where the shark bit with a flap taken from my right leg. I was quite excited about my new skinny legs. All was going well but for some reason that we're not sure of, suddenly yesterday my flap started to die. In the end, they had to remove it (my flap, not my leg). That means I'm back to square one. Major setback but that means there's only one direction to head … forward. I'll rest for a few days then go back to the OR and start over again.

Since I'm back to square one, that makes today a new beginning and a better beginning since we're experienced now. ☺

I'll try to keep posting updates as I imagine they help all of you who are concerned but unable to talk to me.

Hope everyone has a wonderful day.

Categories: Uncategorized | 28 Comments

February 16th, 2011.

Posted on February 16, 2011 by Nicole Moore

OK, so check out the amazing day I had ...

I had a great visit with Laura B this morning, who was lucky enough to arrive in time for my a.m. bath. I'm not sure if she'll ever look at me the same again. Only special friends get to see me THAT up close and personal. ☺

Jay, my dad & my aunt (who flew here from Italy after my ordeal) came for a visit and brought me lunch so I was even spared from hospital food. How lucky am I.

I sent a text to a friend of mine who's a grade one teacher and said "hi" to her class via the message, and apparently the class thinks I'm something to get excited about making me feel just tickled pink.

Here's the big news ... I just finished my first physio session!!! That makes it a great day in itself. Big plans tomorrow ... I'm going to try to get up to a chair for the first time in over 2 weeks. A little apprehensive but looking forward to it.

And my day's not even over yet. Teri, AKA the queen of torture, is coming for a visit shortly & bringing me dinner tonight too. Again, I get to miss the torture of hospital food a have great company. Can this day get any better? The simplest things make me so happy these days and what is more important than good friends & family, love, good food, children's laughter and good health?

Hope every else had a good day too.

Categories: Uncategorized | 35 Comments

Hi

Posted on February 18, 2011 by Nicole Moore

2 days and no posts. Bet some of you are worrying but no need. Things are going great, just really busy and tiring. I hope to post my most recent events later this eve but wanted to throw this post out quickly so people know that nothing is wrong.

Cheers

Categories: Uncategorized | 4 Comments

February 18th, 2011

Posted on February 19, 2011 by Nicole Moore

How about an update …

I'm in great spirits. Not unusual you say? Maybe not, after all I do believe in positive thinking because negativity only breeds negativity, but there is something that I think is important to share with you all.

Monday was a really bad day for me. For two weeks after my shark attack, I gave my all, enduring so much suffering, to gain steps forward in my healing. But in one day (Monday), all of the surgeries and all of my battles were reduced to nothing and my injuries were basically back to the state that they were in just after the attack. Back to square one. I was devastated. I broke down, cried, felt helpless and scared. I had a quiet day that day. Tuesday morning, when I woke, I told myself that it's a new day & that I need to move forward, but my heart was not on board with this plan. It was still too heavy with sadness … until I opened my blog page. I saw the incredible response to my "bad day" posting and was overwhelmed. Seeing all of the responses and reading all of the comments made me feel so supported and loved that it gave me the strength I needed to carry me through that bad day.

People have told me that my story and my attitude are inspirational, yet to me, the response from everyone else is what I find inspirational. Much of my strength and attitude stems from the love and support of my family and friends. If you feel helpless, like you wish you could do more, please take my words to heart when I tell you that you're giving me the most valuable gift anyone could give me … love and for that I am grateful.

Moving on with the update …

People kept telling me how gorgeous it was outside today but I couldn't tell from my hospital bed. The view is comical. If you look out my hospital window, it's like I'm in a prison infirmary but for good behavior, got a view of the prison's exercise block. I can't see sky or any other part of nature.

So, I got up to a wheelchair and my wonderful husband & my family wheeled me around the hospital and I was able to go outside briefly to get a breath of fresh air. I was elated. Yes … up to a chair!! We accomplished this yesterday for the first time & I didn't even pass out although I was a little lightheaded and Jay said I looked a little pale. It's such an incredible joy for me to get out of bed.

Physio also connected a monkey bar set to my bed, aka bed cradle, so that I can move around more in bed. Another bonus but Jay said I'm going to develop an "Arnie" right arm after all of this. Maybe Hollywood will want to design a transformer character after me since they all have weapons built into their arms. Any name suggestions?

Hope everyone got a chance to enjoy this weather too.

As far as my rehab goes, my incredible surgical team are planning how to move forward with my leg and arm. I am scheduled to return to surgery Tuesday morning and that surgery will greatly determine the next course of action. We are going day by day at this point, not knowing how I'll feel daily, taking it easy and limiting visitors. I know you understand that I need time to heal, but I do wish I could see you all.

Lastly, so many people have written incredible sentiments, given incredible gifts, made incredible things and have done outstanding things for me, Jay and the girls that we are quite overwhelmed. It is very hard for us to receive these things, as for us, it is easier to give than receive, but we understand people's desire to help. As a friend pointed out, if it was someone else, we would feel the same way.

We feel a great desire to thank each and every one of you that has given in any form but has proven to be an impossible task. There are just too many thanks to be made. We feel so bad for not being able thank each person individually, but have been told many a time that people understand and do not expect thanks. We hope people do understand and know that your kindness and generosity are not unnoticed or taken for granted. Please accept a HUGE THANKS en masse for all of the selfless things you have done to ease our suffering.

The world is a better place because of all of you.

Categories: Uncategorized | 27 Comments

Happy Long Weekend.

Posted on February 20, 2011 by Nicole Moore

I'm writing this from my hotrod wheelchair in the cafeteria with my devoted and loving driver Jay. What a spectacle we are. Imagine this … An athletic, tall, dark and extremely handsome man taking his petite wife in a wheelchair for a walk. Sounds beautiful right? Here's the spectacle part: I have 2 IV pumps, so many IV bags that it looks like a tree of spaghetti, a PCA pump, 2 vac dressings with a vac pump and a catheter, not to mention all of the dressings. Most of you won't know what half of that stuff is but it's a lot of stuff and it's all attached to an IV pole and this little wheelchair. It's a feat trying to push me around the hospital but one that Jay has mastered. People are always turning their heads to look at the bionic woman and her gorgeous sidekick.

Yesterday, Tia & Ella came for a visit with Jay, my dad and my aunt. The girls are asking more and more questions about my injuries, which is great. The more they ask, the less apprehensive they seem. Tia & Ella bring the most beautiful pictures for me when they visit. I have an incredible wall full of art that I love to look at (makes up for the lack of a view) but I'm not sure the hospital shares my enthusiasm since we're maiming the hospital wall with pinholes. Too bad.

Quiet day today. Jay & I are hanging out relaxing. Isn't that what long weekends are all about. The cold may have returned but the sun is shining like a summer day. Hope that each of you gets to spend some family time together and do something fun.

Categories: Uncategorized | 25 Comments

Family Day

Posted on February 21, 2011 by Nicole Moore

I was just heading off to sleep before my big day tomorrow and thought I'd check the blog. WOW!! Thanks so much for all of the incredible support from everyone. It really gives me strength.

The kids visited today and I was able to surprise them at the elevator in my chair. I was hoping to post a pic of it but I'm technically challenged and could not do it. I'll keep working at it for another day. It was a great day. I hope everyone had a good family day and continues the spirit of the day throughout the year.

My surgery tomorrow could be a couple of hours or another 13 hours like before depending on what they see when they remove my bandages. I love and believe in my surgical team here and feel that I am in good hands. That, combined with all of the love & support I have from my friends and family, makes me feel ready for the operation. When I'm feeling up to it, I'll post a message to let you all know how well the surgery went.

In the mean time, live well, laugh often, love much.

Categories: Uncategorized | 14 Comments

The Good, The Bad, The Ugly

Posted on February 22, 2011 by Nicole Moore

Today's operation over and it was only a couple a hours. I'm exhausted but wanted to give an update. There is good news and bad.

The good news is that my legs are doing better than we had hoped for. My own tissue is growing and filling in some of the bite site. That means I have a better chance that the next flap (a piece of my tissue used to cover the wound) will survive and a better recovery.

Now the bad news …

My left arm has been the more challenging of the two wounds and we were hoping that we could nurture it and continue with the slow reconstruction. Today, however, when they removed my dressing, the damage had worsened. Unfortunately, my arm cannot be saved and will be amputated on Friday.

I am saddened by this news but I am alive and that is far more important. It will take a lot of adjustment, but I know I can get through this like so many other people. If I falter along the way, I know that I have many people wanting and willing to lend a hand and help me through. I am blessed.

I'm falling asleep as I'm writing this so its time for me rest. Good night.

Categories: Uncategorized | 39 Comments

A little change

Posted on February 23, 2011 by Nicole Moore

I met with the orthopedic surgeon that was to be doing my surgery but she is unable to do it on Friday. I don't have a reschedule date for my amputation as of yet but I'll keep you posted.

Today we had a nice family dinner all together at the hospital and we explained to the girls that mommy's arm was too broken and that they have to take it off, and with time give me a new one. We were worried about this conversation but it went really well. Kids are amazing … especially mine. ☺

Categories: Uncategorized | 36 Comments

Problem with Server — Have a Great Weekend

Posted on February 25, 2011 by Nicole Moore

I'm not ignoring you all. We are having issues with our server and are finding it difficult to get on the blog. The only new news I have is that I stood today and transferred to a chair on my feet for the first time. They have been using a lift to get me up to the chair until today. I'm getting there guys! I have no new news about my amputation date and won't have any until Monday so I don't expect that I'll post anything over the weekend. I'll try to post Monday late afternoon once I've seen all my docs. So until then, have a great weekend filled with so much laughter that your face hurts. ☺

Categories: Uncategorized | 19 Comments

Meaningful Quote

Posted on February 27, 2011 by Nicole Moore

A friend of mind has been bugging me to post an inspirational quote that means something to me. There are so many quotes that I'm inspired by but that haven't felt right for this journey in my life ... until I read this on the Academy Awards:

> "It's not the load that breaks you,
> It's the way you carry it."
> Lena Horne

Categories: Uncategorized | 8 Comments

Every Day Heroes

Posted on February 28, 2011 by Nicole Moore

I sent this to a friend who was facing a very challenging recovery. My friend sent it back to me today, encouraging my recovery. I wanted to share it with everyone since we all need a little encouragement.

> Everyday Heroes
> There are all kinds of heroes who live in this world,
> all kinds of heroes we meet —
> They are there in our circle of family and friends
> And the strangers we pass on the street.
> There are heroes who somehow find strength to go on
> even when they feel weary inside,
> And heroes whose gift is their honest emotion,
> the truth of the tears they have cried.
> There are heroes whose courage saves people and nations,
> who search out the safe path ahead,
> And heroes whose job is to quietly listen
> or tuck a small child into bed.

There are everyday heroes who touch our hearts deeply
without even knowing they do,
There are heroes around us wherever we go-
there's a hero right now within you.

Categories: Uncategorized | 14 Comments

Good News, Bad News, No News

Posted on February 28, 2011 by Nicole Moore

I know that everyone is on pins 'n needles checking the blog for some
kind of update so here it is. Sorry that the news is coming so late but
hopefully, better late than never. The good news is I got the surgeon that
I wanted. The bad news is I have to have an above the elbow amputation.
I was hoping we could stay below the elbow but there's no way around it
unless a miracle happens. The no news part is I don't have a date for the
amputation yet. In the mean time, we are going ahead with a planned
surgery tomorrow (Tuesday).

So how am I doing? Good. I'm OK with this plan and hoping the
surgery is sooner than later so I can move forward.

A lot of people have asked me how I can be OK with all of this and
handle it so well. My answer is:

I'm healthy, I'm strong, I'm alive. (Right, Stacey?)

I'm motivated to face the difficulties in my recovery with a positive
attitude because I can.

When I know a surgery date for my amputation, I'll post it because
based on the outpouring of comments, I know how many of you care.
I may sound like a broken record, but I am truly touched by all of the
support I have received from so many on this blog, in our community
and beyond. Thank you to all of you. You lift my spirits.

Categories: Uncategorized | 20 Comments

I Hate Tuesdays

Posted on March 1, 2011 by Nicole Moore

A negative title … first hint not Nicole writing this. It is her husband, Jay. Nicole asked me to add a post for her as she is not up to it today.

I used to like Tuesdays … cheap night at the movies … family night … now it has become surgery night, and to be candid it really, really sucks. Today Nicole had her leg operated on for the umpteenth time and unfortunately this has been one of her worst pain days so far. The hard part is we are not sure why … not to worry anyone, as the doctors don't seem concerned and the surgery went as planned. I am sure we will get through tonight but I don't do it with the same strength and grace as Nicole.

Nicole wanted me to let all of you know that she is on the waiting list for her amputation tomorrow, which she has made peace with and wants to move forward …

I would like all of you to read a quote that I thought personified my wife prior to this horrific incident and now have been proven 100% correct:

"Anyone can give up, it is the easiest thing in the world to do. But to hold it together when everyone else would understand and expect you to fall apart … that is the strength we should all aspire to achieve."

Categories: Uncategorized | 16 Comments

The Day After

Posted on March 2, 2011 by Nicole Moore

Franklin D. Roosevelt said, "If you come to the end of your rope, tie a knot and hang on."

Whew … We made it through yesterday and today is a much better day. My pain is under control now, Jay is smiling again, and everything is brighter.

My amputation was cancelled for today (yay ... I can eat again) and rescheduled for Friday. I wanted to get the operation done and out of the way so that I could move forward in my recovery, but I'm not disappointed. It's a blessing really. This way, I have time to sort out my leg pain and get comfortable before the next surgery and Jay can focus on helping the Law Enforcement All-Stars kick the NHL Alumni's butt tomorrow. I'm still moving forward with my recovery ... just a little slower at this time. Slow and steady gets the job done too, right?

We are still having trouble with the server and I apologize to those of you who have been having trouble posting comments. It has also made it difficult for me to moderate and post your messages but hopefully, we'll work it out soon.

My loving father, who spent the night with me to make sure that the nurses & docs kept on their toes and looked after his little girl adequately, has gone home & I am having a quiet day with Jay today. He's napping right now and I'll likely be doing the same soon. Hope everyone is having a great Wednesday.

Categories: Uncategorized | 27 Comments

Operation Day

Posted on March 4, 2011 by Nicole Moore

Good news ... the docs told me that I'm next on the list and should be in the OR in about an hour.

At this point they are still not sure if they can amputate below the elbow or above. It will take a miracle along with some creative thinking on the side of my determined surgical team to make a below amputation happen but I always say hope for the best, plan for the worst ... I know you will all be thinking of me ... I will post as soon as I am able after the surgery.

Categories: Uncategorized | 9 Comments

In Recovery Mode

Posted on March 4, 2011 by Nicole Moore

Hey … Jay again. Nicole is in recovery after surgery and I am told every-thing went as planned … I don't feel that it is my right to post anything other than that until Nicole is awake and able to post her own com-ments … thanks again to all of you who attended the hockey game and assisted with the raffle toward Nicole's awesome prosthetic … now we move forward.

Categories: Uncategorized | 7 Comments

One Step Closer to Home

Posted on March 5, 2011 by Nicole Moore

Good morning. And what a good morning it is.

Outside it's a little dreary but for me it's a bright and sunny day. My operation is over and it went as planned. The amputation unfortunately was above the elbow, but honest to goodness, when I woke up, I was so happy it was over that I almost started giggling. I was grinning ear to ear and making jokes. When it was time for me to leave the recovery room, the lady that was next to me said, "Do you really have to go?"

When I look at my bandaged stump, oddly enough, it reminds me of a hedgehog. So now me and my hedgehog can move on …

One step closer to home & one step closer to being home with my wonderful girls Tia Bia and Jelly Bean.

This morning I am a little groggy as we are still working out the right combination of pain control medication. Jay is having a grand old time watching me as I fell asleep while drinking my milk (just about giving myself a milk bath) and reaching for my coffee but missing it cuz I'm seeing double. ☺ The grogginess is passing quickly and I should be up to having visitors. I should have surgery on Tuesday for my leg (bad Tuesdays again) which, if all goes well, will be the final surgery during this stay in hospital. My only focus after Tuesday is physio, physio, physio.

If anyone wants to come visit me just let me know. I would love to see you all … just not all at once.

You can contact me by using the "contact" tab at the top of my blog page (thanks Danny boy) which sends a message automatically to my email. If you're having issues using the contact tab, you can text me.

Put on your water wings for the record rainfall and enjoy it. It's only a dreary day if you want it to be … it's all about attitude. ☺

Categories: Uncategorized | 36 Comments

Sunday Evening

Posted on March 6, 2011 by Nicole Moore

No new medical news to report. We are still trying to get the right pain control formula otherwise I'm still doing OK with my stump. I am, however, exhausted most of the time, so please excuse any mistakes.

I had a wonderful day today filled with lots of terrific visitors including my precious girls who were busy at the grandparents all weekend long making T-shirts, exquisite artwork, and scrapbooks that brought tears to my eyes. To top things off, they each gave me a necklace that was a heart and a key. They gave me one half and I have the others … "that way," Tia said, "you'll always have the key to my heart." Even my niece Hayden came (3 hours away) to present me with the best hairbands ever that she and her brother had made. It just doesn't get any better than this. This is why I'm grateful to be alive at any cost.

Except shift workers, I'll bet most other people are just getting ready to sit on the couch, flick on the TV, and relax. That's exactly what I'm about to do. Movie night with my dad.

Categories: Uncategorized | 11 Comments

Surgery postponed

Posted on March 7, 2011 by Nicole Moore

Finally time to sit and blog. These days I feel like I have no me time but at the same time, I love all the visits. I'll find the happy medium.

So what about my surgery???

My surgeons told me that they are happy with how my leg is doing so they want to wait another few days. So the next and hopefully the last operation is now scheduled for Friday instead.

There was also some rambling about a discharge plan, which puts a grin on my face (one step closer) but that is so far off that I'll just keep my focus on day by day.

Another big day today filled with lots of great visitors.

I met a woman today that has been an extraordinary help to my family. She has done so much including organizing the auction at the old timers hockey game that words cannot express our gratitude. Sincere thanks to our angel Val. I loved meeting you.

Laura & Sabrina came this morning (I made sure my bath was finished this time ☺) and were here when physio came. They were able to witness me getting out of bed and watched as I stood again. Keep in mind that I haven't stood since February 18th and I stood right up!!! It's funny isn't it? Most of you get up on your legs to get somewhere and never think about doing it, but to me it's a huge accomplishment. It'll get easier for me, but I hope I continue to take pleasure in the little things.

I also lost my hedgehog today. The ortho doc came and removed my big furry dressing thus taking away my hedgehog ... yes it was hard to lose her, but I got through it. ☺I am left with just a simple dressing over the stump and it looks more normal now.

Life is interesting at times but it's life and I love it.

A little bit of understanding

Posted on March 9, 2011 by Nicole Moore

I suppose most of you have seen the story of me published today in the *Toronto Star*. I feel compelled to mention that I did not condone this story. I found out about it by sheer coincidence yesterday and told them that I didn't want them to run it. Although the story was well written and not malicious, it still did two things that I was not prepared for at this time; it made my blog global and opened the gate releasing the media lions. The response from people and reporters is staggering. I thought it was difficult keeping up with the blog before today but now I am completely overwhelmed. As a result, I don't believe that I'll be able to keep up with responses in a timely manner and that I'll have even less time to return comments or messages. This breaks my heart. I love, appreciate, and draw strength from your postings and I want to reply to each one. I know it's not expected, but in my heart, I truly want to. This was an impossible task prior to today but I was able to respond to some at least. Now that the blog has gone global and based on the volumes of blogs and messages that I witnessed today, at this time I will not be able to respond to many people so ...

I'm asking for a little understanding when I am unable to get to your postings, messages, email, texts, etc. in a timely manner or when I'm unable to post a message. I'll do what I can when I can but my recovery is what I must focus on first. I know you'll understand.

I want to welcome and send thanks out to the new people that have started to read my blog. I hope you're inspired by not only my story, but more importantly by the people that respond. I hope that readers read each others' comments as they can easily raise you up close to heaven and make your day brighter.

If media is reading this and wish to contact me, I respectfully request that you do not burden me, my family or friends with more messages or phone calls. I am willing to give into requests but ask that the requests go through Laura or Craig at the Communications and Stakeholder Relations department at Sunnybrook (416 480 4040) so that I can focus on my recovery.

Thanks to all for what I hope will be a little bit of understanding.

A very exhausted girl wishes all of you good night and I'll post as soon as I can.

Categories: Uncategorized | 69 Comments

One more to go!

Posted on March 11, 2011 by Nicole Moore

Before I head off to sleep, I wanted to say thanks for so many well wishes and prayers for my surgery. I very well could be the most blessed person undergoing surgery.

I'm looking forward to finishing what should be the last surgery of this hospital stay. If all goes well, then I can focus on going home.

I'll let you know how it went as soon as possible.

Categories: Uncategorized | 12 Comments

The Summit

Posted on March 11, 2011 by Nicole Moore

I did it.

I faced the mountain ahead of me, all shredded & torn. Something inside of me knew I had to reach the other side and so I climbed, step by step, always looking up and moving forward.

Today I reached the summit ... the last operation on the road toward home, and conquered it.

I know the path down the mountain can be arduous, but with the summit behind me, I am driven by a sense of fulfillment which eases the doubt.

I have so many people supporting my journey but there is one group that I owe endless thanks to and that is to the tireless efforts of my surgical team lead by the wonderful Dr. Snell. My wounds were unimaginable ... kinda like Humpty Dumpty, but unlike all of Mexico's horses and all of Mexico's men, she and her team put me together again. ☺

Categories: Uncategorized | 37 Comments

And The Silence Is Broken...

Posted on March 15, 2011 by Nicole Moore

It's a bright sunny Tuesday and no surgery. I'm already starting the day off right. I also have another reason to be excited. Since my last surgery, I've been on strict bedrest which has been driving me crazy but if all goes well, tomorrow should be my last day of bedrest.

My last operation involved taking skin grafts from my good leg and transplanting them to my bite leg. This type of operation is very delicate, but even more so with me because I don't have the tissue base on the recipient site that normal people have so I have to stay very still in bed (shhhh, be verwy, verwy, quiet ... I'm huntin rwabbit). Tomorrow, the docs will remove my dressing and see if the graft took. If it looks good then I can start to rehab slowly on Thursday. If the graft didn't take ... well, let's not think like that.

So in keeping with my mountain theme, it's kinda like I'm sitting on the top of the mountain, enjoying the view but anxiously awaiting permission to start the descent. I can't wait until tomorrow.

Passing the past few days of bedrest has been the greatest. I have devoted a tremendous amount of time reading the massive amount of email that I have received. The messages are amazing. Most are filled with heartfelt get well wishes, love, and prayers, others are filled with other people's stories of struggle and triumph. I have received messages from all around the world. It's unfortunate that many of these messages came to my email instead of posting on the blog as many of them are truly inspirational. I loved reading them and appreciate the support. The other thing that has made the last few days awesome is March Break. I have been able to spend hours each day with my kids. There are no words to express the joy that my children bring me. I can't wait to be home.

I was looking back through my blog and realized that I never wrote about the wonderful hockey game that took place. Every year the NHL Alumni challenge the Law Enforcement All-Stars to a hockey game in Orangeville. This event raises money for charity. A woman by the name of Val Burke and her husband Dale took it upon themselves to organize a raffle with the assistance of the Orangeville Optimist Club and many other sponsors to raise money for me. This raffle took place during this hockey game. My husband played in the game and my children walked out onto a red carpet to draw the raffle winners. They felt famous. I, of course, could not be there but have seen the video and have heard from many people that the whole event was incredible. I can't thank Val & Dale enough for their tremendous efforts and their endless support. They are wonderful and selfless people … especially because I had never met them prior to this event. All of the money raised is going toward the purchase of my prosthesis.

So many other people have collected, raised, or simply donated money and gifts to assist us in this difficult time and we are so touched and honored to be part of such a giving society. I am blown away by people's generosity. What a wonderful world we live in.

I hope everyone is enjoying their week. I will post again soon letting you know if I am free to run.

Categories: Uncategorized | 19 Comments

Thumbs Up

Posted on March 16, 2011 by Nicole Moore

Is everyone sitting on the edge of their seats biting their nails waiting for a response?? Almost all of the people close to me have called or text me cuz they had to find out what the docs said.

Well here it is … they said let's wait until Thursday or Friday.

I was so disappointed and verbalized it, perhaps too much, but to my relief, my wonderful Dr. folded. She removed my dressing (making me pay for my persuasion through pain) and all is well. The grafts took.

I have to be on bedrest for 2 more days and then another 2 more days of just dangling my legs off the edge of the bed but then I have the thumbs up to slowly move onto physio. I can begin to learn how to walk again but the doc put some reins on me however. I will not be able to weight bear for 4 weeks on by bite leg so I'll have to learn how to walk with a device of some sort. A challenge without an arm but together with physio, we have begun to brainstorm on some ideas already and will

MacGyver something together. My doctors really stressed that I have to take it slow or I may damage the leg and set me back dramatically. Despite my surging desire to push as hard as I can to get out of here, I will take heed of their advice so don't expect me to blog huge accomplishments. It'll be baby steps but as I said before ... slow and steady still gets the job done ... but I'll still be pushing the envelope on those baby steps. ☺

If you were waiting for the update on the seat of your pants, I apologize for the tardiness of this message.

Mountain descent commencing in T-4 days. Gear up!

Categories: Uncategorized | 13 Comments

Happy St. Patrick's Day

Posted on March 17, 2011 by Nicole Moore

Just wanted to wish everyone a happy St. Patrick's day. A gorgeous, warm, sunny day worth celebrating. In fact, since I'm half Irish (my mum was born in Ireland) I'm having a little sip of beer as I write. Don't fret, it's just a sip and why not? Even if you're not Irish, why not try to find something big or small, to celebrate in your own way.

Celebrate when you can. Just ask any Japanese or Liberian.

Cheers

Categories: Uncategorized | 9 Comments

Dingle Dangle Days

Posted on March 20, 2011 by Nicole Moore

March break is over and I can hear the cheers of parents in the streets, but I, for one, will miss spending quality time with my husband and my kids. I am however, cheering for different reasons ...

Hooray ... My bedrest is over!! Over the weekend, in between my plethora of visitors, I have been dangling my feet over the side of the bed a little bit at a time. I was also able to get up to my wheelchair yesterday and today. Yes, I said wheelchair not hotrod. I guess I forgot to mention that both of my vac machines are gone along with my PCA pump and my IV pumps. You might not understand what all of that is, but what matters is that a lot of what I needed to get better is not needed anymore and is gone. Without all of the fantastic parts, my wheelchair now looks just like a wheelchair and that's it. I'm light as a feather!! ☺ Tomorrow is a big day. I get to get up with physio. Maybe I'll just stand and pivot to a chair or maybe we'll just hobble a few steps (no weight bear on bad leg for 4 weeks). Either way, I'll be up and I couldn't be happier. These little advances mean so much to me. To me, each achievement is a pat on my back and on the backs of my health care team and my family.

Family or not, March break or not, I hope that last week made you thankful for something and that this week you're just as lucky.

Categories: Uncategorized | 20 Comments

Close But Not Out the Door Yet

Posted on March 22, 2011 by Nicole Moore

OMG … I walked out of my room and down the hall … but not out of the door yet. I'm making spectacular advancements if I do say so myself, but now I see that I have a long way to go. Let me back up a bit.

Yesterday was the first day that I was officially allowed to do full physio. So here I am all gung-ho and chomping at the bit to execute MY plan of action when along comes my awesome but practical physiotherapist who is quick to put on the reigns and veto MY plan.

The nerve of the professional to know what's right for me!! Just kidding. Bonnie, my physiotherapist, wanted to make sure I was safe and that my muscles were ready and I agreed. And so we started what was to be a slow introduction to walking. Fortunately, each movement that she guided me through was accomplished swiftly until I was taking small steps … a task that Bonnie was surprised I accomplished. I learned how to balance on a crutch and took about 5 steps to my wheelchair. Up until now, I have only stood, pivoted and shuffled a bit to my chair. These were my first real steps. I wonder if toddlers, when they are learning to walk and have just taken their first steps, feel as proud and great as I felt? That was day one.

Today, day two, I am officially tube free. No more IV lines (PICC lines for you nurses out there that understand) and no more catheter. Nothing.

Being tube free, I accomplished two major things: I peed on a toilet for the first time (sorry but it's SUCH a great feeling when you haven't done it in forever!) again I wonder if a successful toilet training toddler feels the same way, and I walked. Bonnie and I started out with the goal of trying to walk with my crutch to the door of my bathroom but when I got there — what did Forest Gump say? "(I) figured, since I'd gone this far, I might as well … just keep on going," so I walked out of my room and all the way to the nurse's station. Ka-ching!!! Jay wasn't with me yesterday so to see me walk at all, much less this distance, amazed him, he said. A huge accomplishment and I am proud of myself but I also realized how weak my muscles are and how far I still have to go. I still have a long descent, but I'm loving the view so far. ☺ Upon some solid recommendations, I have agreed to go to a rehab facility to continue my care. At this point, I don't know when and where I'll be going but I hope to know soon. Unfortunately, it will not be closer to home. ☹ The type of facility that I need is only offered here in Toronto, so here I stay. Despite the move, I'm still going to try to be home for my birthday. I've made it this far so I'm going to just keep pushing and giving my all. I know no other way.

Buckle up … here I come.

Categories: Uncategorized | 43 Comments

Out the Door But Not Home Yet

Posted on March 25, 2011 by Nicole Moore

I was making such leaps and bounds with my physio that Sunnybrook decided I was too healthy to stay but not healthy enough to go home yet. I have left the hospital and went to a rehab facility. I am excited because the place is so much more comfortable and 100% geared toward physio. I'm walking well but am still incredibly weak so this place is exactly what I need. Here's the bad news … the rehab centre does not have Wi-fi. Can you believe it? I have become so accustomed to it that I was left dumbfounded wondering what I'm going to do. I guess I can find things to do to fill my time but I will not be able to blog as often. ☹ There is a computer with internet access available but it is shared with the rest of the residents so it won't be that often. I have been here for 6 hours already and this is the first time I have seen the computer free. Anyone having flashbacks of home and fighting over something with a brother or sister? Of course this means that it will take me much longer to post your comments and even longer to post again. I will try to get on and post any other big accomplishments as they come. All and all, I don't expect that I will be here very long ... two weeks at the most, but we'll see. The difficult part of the downhill path begins now but I'm so close to completing my journey. Time to dig my heels in and get to work.

Categories: Uncategorized | 14 Comments

Una Piccola Nota Per Gli Amici Italiani

Posted on March 28, 2011 by Nicole Moore

Ho ricevuto molti meravigliosi messaggi dagli amici italiani senza avere mai rilasciato notizie nella loro lingua e voglio prendere l'opportunità di correggermi.

Sono in una clinica di riabilitazione dove mi sto "allenando" per il mio ritorno a casa che dovrebbe avvenire presto. È con vero sollievo vedere che sto recuperando molte delle mie funzioni guadagnando una discreta indipendenza. Sono stata molto sorpresa e veramente commossa dall' incredibile supporto ricevuto dall'Italia. Sapevo di avere grandissimi amici, ma non mi aspettavo una prova di affetto così forte. Le vostre parole sono state di molto aiuto e vi ringrazio di cuore.

Spero di vedervi di persona a Settembre.

Ciao a tutti.

Categories: Uncategorized | 2 Comments

Life at Rehab

Posted on March 28, 2011 by Nicole Moore

Hi everyone! I figured it out … dinner arrived to our rooms and instead of eating I went to the lounge. Kaching! A free computer. Yes, people eat the food here, including myself. Alas, the days of mystery food are behind me along with the lovely hospital smells. I'm at St. John's Rehab. For those of you that are familiar with the place, IT'S OLD!!! I feel like I passed through some wormhole and ended up in the 40s but the gardens are gorgeous, even in sprinter (the period between spring & winter). Nuns from the neighbouring convent walk the halls, ready to talk to anyone who needs an ear. Here, that means just about everyone. 10 minutes in the lounge and you've heard about 5 different horrific accidents and several debates about whose injuries are worse and why. It's amazing … kinda like happy hour at the old age home with echoes of residents comparing aches & illnesses.

I like this place. I really miss the staff at Sunnybrook, but there is so much more freedom here and it's peaceful. More importantly, it's the final stepping stone toward home. I haven't had a lot of physio yet but I'm growing stronger & stronger each day. The best part of my day was getting plastered. No, not drinking (how many of you raised your eyebrows briefly in dismay?), I mean with actual plaster. My upper body was first wrapped in panty hose, then wrapped in Saran wrap (don't ask). After that, plaster was slathered on my left upper arm, rubbed, formed and smoothed it until it formed a hard cast. This cast of my stump will be used to make a mold of my arm for the beginning stages of my prosthetic development. Exciting! I met an amazing woman last week named Kelly who is also an upper arm amputee. She generously gave up her time to visit me and teach me about prostheses, gadgets available to help with tasks, need-to-know tricks and how being an amputee is easier than I thought. She left me with an even greater sense of hope and inspiration. Thanks, Kelly.

So far life has been alright at rehab but I'm waiting anxiously for the workout to begin. Have you worked out this week?

Categories: Uncategorized | 23 Comments

There's No Place Like Home

Posted on April 7, 2011 by Nicole Moore

One girls trip (+1 guy) to Cancun disrupted by a shark attack, two land and one air ambulance, 3 hospitals, 6 teams of surgeons, 8 surgeries, 1 amputation, 127 nurses, 141 mystery hospital meals, 24 blood product transfusions, a kazillion medications and 100% determination.

Being home before expected date of discharge ... PRICELESS!!!

Yes, I'm home and I cannot adequately express in words the feeling of serenity and joy upon walking through that door. I have made it over the mountain and landed in paradise. Children's hugs and giggles, peaceful night sleeps, healthier food, comforting company. The healing of my body is almost over ... now I've started the healing of my mind and soul.

I came home on April first, April fool's day. I didn't tell my kids that I was coming home because I wanted to surprise my kids and boy did we ever achieve it. When the kids came home from school, Jay told them that he had a surprise for them and that it was something that they have been asking for for months but they'd have to find it first. He sent them looking all over half the house and when they were getting frustrated because they couldn't find it, he yelled "April Fool's Day!!" The kids were super disappointed as you can imagine (they thought they were getting the Nintendo DS that they have been begging for). Then Jay sent the whining kids to the kitchen, where I was waiting, to put their school stuff away as they always do. When they turned the corner into the kitchen, they saw me, dropped their bags, yelled "mommy's home" and came running to me. Again, tears were falling. It was wonderful and they have been very loving and helpful ever since.

I'm walking with a crutch on my right side (obviously) and I have a brace on my left leg, which was put there 4 weeks ago to protect the skin graft. The brace comes off on the 13th and I should begin to walk using both legs but I will need lots of physio to relearn how to walk properly. I have also been keeping up with the prosthetic team and will continue to do so. I'll be doing my physiotherapy, occupational therapy and prosthetics at Sunnybrook. Sadly, due to budgetary cutbacks and poor insight, there is no longer OHIP covered physio at Headwaters hospital (our local hospital) nor in the surrounding areas. The closest one available to me was Brampton (1/2 hour away), however, the OT was not willing to take me as a pt due to the complexity of my case (?????). That meant that I'd have to travel to Toronto for my OT anyways, so I decided to do all my therapy there.

I'm sorry for taking so long to post a message but when I got home, and could finally get internet service, I wanted some quiet time with my family and to get adjusted to being home again.

Now I have updated my second family … all of you that have supported me throughout this journey. I am sending out my warmest wishes for good health, love and happiness to all of you along with my deepest thanks.

Categories: Uncategorized | 32 Comments

What a beautiful day

Posted on April 10, 2011 by Nicole Moore

Here in Orangeville, where the snow just let out despite persistently low temps and generally miserable weather, it was an absolutely gorgeous day. The temp was only around 15 degrees Celsius but with a beaming sun, pure blue skies, and only a gentle breeze, it felt like paradise to me. Days like today draw people outside. Maybe to do the run that's been put off all winter or go for a walk, wash the car, clean the garage or just sit and enjoy it. Anything just to get out. Young and old pass by and wave or stop to chat. Slow as I am these days of adapting to my new one armed life, I was eager to get outside this morning and catch up with my kids who had already gone outside well before me. I think all of my neighbours were out. Some of you at this point would cringe and do anything to avoid talking to some of them but I am really fortunate as I have the greatest neighbours and many of us are also friends. Being away for so long, it was really nice to see them and catch up with their lives and of course update them with my eventful last few months. We put up our trampoline this weekend so our kids are in jumping heaven since they've been asking just about every day since I've been home. In the afternoon, my in-laws came for a visit. Again, some of you may cringe, even run and hide and do anything to avoid them, but I'm lucky that I don't have the typical monster in-laws. In fact, I have the greatest in-laws in the world and they are also the best Grandma & Grandpa EVER!! They came by (a mere 250 km drive) to see how I was doing and to show the girls the baby chicks and baby ducklings that they had just bought for the farm. Soooo cute and a true symbol of spring. The girls were delighted to hold the soft baby birds even if they pooped all over them. The rest of the day I spent sitting in the back yard relaxing and watching my kids jump and play while my husband did the yard work. The end of a perfect day. And even if it rains tomorrow, as they are calling for, my day will still be warmed by the sun of today and from simple perfections.

Categories: Uncategorized | 22 Comments

Time is Precious . . . and so is Nicole

Posted on April 18, 2011 by Nicole Moore

Hello to all you blog addicts, it's Jay hacking in again … I will attempt to minimize any concerns people may have by letting you know that Nicole is doing amazingly well … like any of you would have thought otherwise. Now that she has returned home it seems that her time is very limited and as such she has had little time to post anything as of late.

Last week was a busy one. Nicole celebrated her birthday with a wonderful dinner and our whole family, kids included, attended an amazing fundraiser for Nicole at the Boston Pizza in Orangeville. It was truly unbelievable what support all of our friends have provided to Nicole and our family. Nicole is making, in my opinion, very quick strides both literally and figuratively. She is throwing the crutch aside and doing laps around the house and of course the shopping mall. Thank you again to all of you for the support you have provided. I am sure Nicole will soon begin to have the time and energy to blog again …

Categories: Uncategorized | 12 Comments

Hi. Remember Me?

Posted on May 5, 2011 by Nicole Moore

10:00 pm and finally sitting down, PJs on and my evening cup of lemon tea. This usually is my calming, peaceful time before heading off to a much needed rest, but not lately. Lately, incompleteness plagues my peace in so many ways. I have so much to do but never seem to get ahead lately. I have had so many wonderful moments, great events, and some frustrations to share with you all but haven't been able to. I've tried. I'd began to write only to be interrupted by connectivity, people or, as was the case most of the time, I'd fall asleep while writing (I actually fell asleep standing while brushing my teeth. That's how tired I've been). After a while, the amount of stuff to share kept mounting, and I'd put it off for when I had "more time." Riiiiight. "More time" never comes in busy lives so I wanted to make a moment to say hi to everyone that cares and has been patiently waiting for an update.

I'm doing great!! Would you expect anything else?

My stump is healed and I've been eagerly working with the prosthetic team to form my first arm. I should have a practice prototype by Monday (pretty fast huh?) The options are incredible and can be overwhelming both in price and selection. Fortunately, due to my amazing friends and the incredible community that I live in, the fantastic fundraising initiatives have made cost less of an issue now. How does one thank an entire community for such an altruistic and generous gift? I'll have to share those stories with you in more depth when it's not so late. It's incredibly heartwarming. My leg is healing really well. We had a setback with the wound at Easter but it's on the mend again. If I didn't have setbacks, I wouldn't have the same perspective. Sometimes being forced backward gives a better view of where you're going. I still have a brace on my leg, but I'm able to walk my kids to the bus and go grocery shopping without a crutch. Not having to use a crutch when you only have one hand opens a whole new world of opportunity for me. I love being home even though it's frustrating for me not to be able to do so many things that I want to do and needing 10 times longer to do the things I still can do. This is temporary, I know, and I welcome the challenge of finding new ways to do things but it is nonetheless frustrating. I love sleeping in my own bed. I love being closer to friends. I love being home with my husband and I'm sooooo loving motherhood!! My girls have been so sweet and supportive, helping any chance they can. I love the time with my dad and my aunt (who has sadly returned to Italy) who have been my main nurses and shoulders to lean on. Jay has returned to work but recently, his line of work, in our town, has it's challenges to put it nicely. His stress level hasn't lessened any … it's increased.

In a nutshell … I'm still moving forward, step by step and loving all that life has to offer.

By the way, I was interrupted by 2 different people so posting this took more than 2 hours … but I stayed awake. ☺

Categories: Uncategorized | 13 Comments

Precious Gifts

Posted on May 25, 2011 by Nicole Moore

I just received a koala bear. Yup … a koala. How cool is that? An Australian "Moore to Life" blog reader named Jane thought I might like a replacement for my lost "hedgehog" and adopted a koala in my name. I just received the adoption certificate today (sorry Jane … a note explained that it was sent in March but due to problems with delivery, it was redirected & only received today) with an exquisite picture of "Lili" who, I must say, is much cuter than my hedgehog was. The story of Baby Lili explained how she was found sick & injured and taken to the "Koala Hospital" where, with much TLC and perseverance, she recovered and was released (sound familiar?) The adoption proceeds went toward the Koala Hospital. A very touching gift that helped others and is also symbolic as Jane writes to me, "this hospital is amazing and the koalas are no less amazing in their determination to heal." Thanks, Jane.

I have received so many gifts since Jan 31 of this year. Be it God's will, my determination, the selfless aid of many people on the beach that day in Cancun and/or the wonderful paramedics, nurses & doctors, I was given the gift of life. Ok, so I was already alive, but, I came so close to dying that day that I consider life a gift. Subsequently, I have so much appreciation for what I have in life, good or bad. That too is a gift I suppose, but the most beautiful and touching gifts which I have received since my attack are the many gifts given in so many ways from friends, family, businesses & strangers that I will never know; Incredible messages & cards with words that love, support & inspire, hand knit comforts that embrace, prayers to guide, flowers to brighten, meals to nourish, donations to ease worries & provide opportunities, precious time given for visits, volunteering & organizing events and countless other gifts. Even this blog is an extraordinary gift from the awesome Dan Van Damme & Family. The immense generosity of these gifts, no matter how big or small a gesture, touch me so deeply that I am often brought to tears. How or why so many care for my wellbeing is beyond me but I am so thankful for it. Thank you to everyone for all of your precious gifts.

Life's precious gifts make me one lucky lady … even if I was attacked by a shark.

Categories: Uncategorized | 5 Comments

Back in the saddle … I mean keyboard

Posted on December 2, 2011 by Nicole Moore

Hello once again. I apologize for my long absence but I have got my blog back up and running. I will attempt to post more often in the coming months and give you an update for those of you still following my story. If you wish to get a sneak peak, you can see me on CBC's *Fifth Estate* this evening, December 2nd, 2011, at 9:00pm. The show re-airs on Sunday at 11:00 pm as well.

Type to you all soon.

Categories: Uncategorized | 17 Comments

A Lot Can Happen in a Year

Posted on February 21, 2012 by Nicole Moore

I can hardly believe it, but yes, it has been a year since my shark attack.

So much has happened, so much achieved, but how does one summarize a year of challenges? I don't know, but I'll try.

Firstly, however, I wish to send out an apology. It has been a long time since I've posted an update on my blog. Many people have told me that they enjoyed my blog & have missed my postings. To those who have been waiting & searching for an update, I apologize. I intended to post the occasional update and started to write a post several times, but it never came to fruition. I wanted to focus on me, my family & my recovery and am glad I did so.

I have physioed my butt off and have been busy trying to regain some lost muscle and mobility. Shortly after coming home, I developed some issues with my knee & shoulder on my affected side. It slowed my recovery & made it more painful but hey, what's a couple more challenges? I am currently walking very well without any aids and hardly have a limp. That's impressive, even to me, considering I'm missing 2 of 4 quadricep muscles & almost 2 of 3 hamstrings. I'm not running yet but hope to one day. Over the summer I was able to swim, walk, climb & kayak. How does one kayak with one arm you ask? A paddle kayak. It was awesome!!! I have mastered the stationary bike and am able to walk some stairs. In fact, I have resumed my aerobic step classes once again with "my chicas" that I went to Mexico with originally. As for my arm, it has not progressed as I had expected. I have a wonderful team working on a prosthetic arm for me. In late spring, they let me take it home & I felt like it was Christmas. I loved having it and adapted to it really well but it caused incredible pain. Being a new amputee, I figured this was to be expected and continued on. Me & my prosthetic team worked hard on finding a solution but in the end, the pain was too much and my stump was swelling. An MRI revealed a couple issues to my affected arm causing the pain and swelling. The prosthetic would have to wait until the stump could be fixed. I have been unable to wear it for 6 months. ☹ Pain has been the biggest problem with the arm but hopefully it will be improved soon.

This takes us to present time. In a couple of hours, I return to hospital for some further operations. One of them being a revision of my stump, which I hope will take care of any issues so I can move forward with my prosthetic. My incredible plastics team will also be reconstructing my leg. They will try once again to create a flap to cover my femur which currently only has a few millimetres of skin covering it. This time they will be taking a muscle from my abdomen and placing it over my femur then cover it with a skin flap from my belly. Medicine absolutely amazes me with the things that can be done. They are major surgeries that basically put me back to where I was a year ago & comes with the price of another long hospital stay, away from my children again, but there are perks too. I have been on an all-you-can-eat diet in order to grow a big enough belly to cover the leg. It's been awesome, especially around Christmas. When they cut out the flap from the belly … instant tummy tuck to fix it. If only they could fix the butt that came with the belly, but I'll work on that later. I'm really going to miss this diet though.

My family have been wonderful & my kids have loved having mommy home. I think I enjoyed being home with them more however, because I was one of the few parents that were sad when summer & Christmas was over and the kids had to return to school.

A lot of people ask me how I've been coping and I must say that I have been very fortunate. I have never had any significant post traumatic stress from the attack and no nightmares. That said, it hasn't been easy either. Adjusting to our new lives has been difficult for the whole family at times, but unconditional love, open communication, placing focus on little accomplishments, and just moving forward helps me. Life goes on no matter what. I believe that we have the choice as to how we are going to face life. Live it or sit back and let it pass you by. I for one say bring it on … I will love you no matter what. I hate to complain & when I want to, I remind myself that I am alive and that is a precious thing.

Since I'll be in hospital for the next few weeks, I will try to post on my blog once again to keep people updated with my recovery.

My operation is scheduled for this morning at 7:00 a.m. and, due to the complexity of it, is expected to be a very long one. I imagine I will be snowed once again with the narcotics (falling asleep in my milk again) but will post an update as soon as I am awake enough to do so.

Welcome back to those who are reading once again. I have missed you too.

Welcome new readers.

Categories: Uncategorized | 6 Comments

Post Surgery Update

Posted on February 28, 2012 by Nicole Moore

Yay, surgery is over and once again I am on the road to recovery.

I had my operation last Tuesday … Almost a week post op!!! This is so important and a huge hurdle overcome. Some of you may remember that last February I had this same surgery to rebuild my leg but the donor site was from my right leg. All was well ("was loving my new skinny legs") but for unknown reasons, the flap rejected 6 days later on Feb 14th. It was a bad day. For the past year, we have been prepping & nurturing the site for this repeat operation using a different donor site. Today was day 6 post op & the flap looks great. Tomorrow, the docs will remove my cast & dressings to take a better look but we are expecting great outcomes. Please pray &/or keep fingers & toes crossed that all is well.

So what exactly did they do?

My plastics team reconstructed my left leg using parts from my abdomen. They removed abdominal muscle and placed it over the femur. They then removed a flap from my tummy to cover the bite area as best as they could. Despite fattening up for this surgery with an all-you-can-eat diet, I apparently still didn't have enough to cover the whole wound. My surgeon cut the largest flap she could then went to close my tummy but realized it is too tight. It is so tight that I am unable to lie flat at this time and must remain in a seated position. I also have to keep my leg elevated so I'm stuck in this poorly executed jackknife position. It's quite funny but hey, I'm not complaining. I have a flat tummy again!!

I have to send out thanks for the millions of offers I received for donor fat. No really … millions offered selflessly give up their personal cushion for me. Sorry that I couldn't take up the offers.

It is truly amazing what medicine can do and I am so thankful for my plastic surgeons, especially Dr. Snell, who have invested, even sacrificed, so much of their time to strive for a successful outcome for me.

I was also to have a stump revision and nerve exploration to my left arm. When the orthopedic surgeon opened my stump, however, he decided he only needed to make one revision which did not involve cutting more bone — which was expected. Whew!! He also decided not do a part of the surgery which I felt was important (a nerve repair) therefore I'm not convinced that my arm pain will be entirely resolved, but at this point, I must give the benefit of doubt to the professionals & will hope that this too will be the end of operations to my arm so that I can move forward with my prosthetic pain free.

I am on total bedrest and expect to be this way for a while. "Joy, oh bliss," she said with sarcasm but willing to do whatever it takes to make the surgeries a success. The original hospital stay was quoted about 6 weeks. I quickly begged for leniency and negotiated 3 weeks in hospital (if all went well) followed by 2–3 weeks bedrest at home.

Since being admitted to my favorite unit at Sunnybrook, things are progressing well. I, of course, hope to accelerate this estimate & my surgeon may agree to 2 weeks hospital stay if everything looks well tomorrow (now today). ☺

How am I feeling? Everything aches this time (like I've been hit by a truck) but far less intense compared to what I had to endure last year so I won't complain. Each day is better than the last. I feel sad to leave my beautiful girls at home while mommy goes away again, sorry for having to put my wonderful husband through this again, guilty to burden my father further even though I know he loves being needed, and frustrated at times that I have to do this again.

BUT … I am alive. I am healthy enough to endure these operations. I am strong enough to recover quickly. I am wise enough to know that even though I feel sad, guilty, sorry & frustrated, that it's ok. I am loved enough to know that nothing else matters.

I am elated that it's over and once again I am on the road to recovery.

Categories: Uncategorized | 8 Comments

No New News

Posted on February 29, 2012 by Nicole Moore

Sorry but I have no new news to report.

The docs removed 2 out of 3 of my tubes yesterday (JP tubes for the nurses following this), but weren't able to take down my dressing, citing no time. They said they'd remove the dressing & the last tube today but we are still waiting. I'm keeping my fingers crossed. Today is not my best day. I feel crappy and my pain worse than usual so I'd like to have the dressing done to brighten my day. I'd really like to sneak a peek at my new leg & see if all is going well.

I'll keep you posted.

Categories: Uncategorized | 0 Comments

Good Girl

Posted on February 29, 2012 by Nicole Moore

All the bandages and tubes are officially out … yay!!!!

My new leg looks fantastic and I am very excited. There is one tiny spot that is necrotic but it appears to be superficial & the team is not too concerned. My wonderful surgeon, however, wants to be extra careful and is being uber conservative with my recovery. Rightfully so, I know, but as most of you know, I like to keep moving forward, not stay stagnant. I want to be home with my family as soon as I can. That said, I'm taking no chances. Sometimes our wants have to take a backseat to our needs. Don't worry … this time I won't push it too hard. I'll be a good girl. ☺

So … it looks like I am going to be extending my stay at Sunnybrook for another two weeks. Let's make a game of it: Let's see how many roommates I can go through. So far I have been here 8 days and I'm on my 3rd roommate. She goes home tomorrow. Any bets on how many roomies I'll have before I go home?

Categories: Uncategorized | 3 Comments

I'm Mobile!!!

Posted on March 1, 2012 by Nicole Moore

I'm up ... I'm up!!!

As I'm writing, I am sitting up in a wheelchair, completely ecstatic. I wasn't sure when I'd be able to get up because after my dressing change yesterday, we were missing a few items to stabilize my new leg. The incredible staff here on C5, despite being super busy as always, pursued on my behalf night & day, to quickly attain the special brace I needed to secure my leg.

No sooner was my leg braced that my awesome nurse Erin & Cliff, her sidekick, had me up to a wheelchair. I am so thankful and happy. As if my day couldn't get any better, it's a snow day for my kids so my kids & family are here visiting. Life is great!

Ready ... set ... go

Categories: Uncategorized | 4 Comments

Apologies

Posted on March 4, 2012 by Nicole Moore

I'm sending out apologies to those who tried to post a response to my blog but then never saw it posted. I have been experiencing some issues with my blog. Most of it due to my lack of technical know-how but some are due to problems which occurred when I switched host companies.

When I looked for comments, my site kept saying there were none. I finally figured out there was an issue & hope I can fix it. Awesome Dan, who set the site up for me initially, is helping so it should be ok now.

I have approved the comments that showed up but am afraid that a few may have been missed. If this is the case, I'm sorry to have missed them & please repost.

I admire all you techies out there who understand all this stuff.

Here's hoping I've got it under control now.

Categories: Uncategorized | 0 Comments

Being A Lucky Person is Only a Matter of Perspective

Posted on March 4, 2012 by Nicole Moore

Are you a half glass empty or a half glass full type of person?

I like to think that I'm an optimistic person. I love optimism and positive thinking. I often say that I'm a lucky person. Yes, I was attacked by a shark, which is incredibly rare, but so is surviving a shark attack. To me … I'm pretty lucky.

When things are difficult, as they've been at the best of times, I can often make it through by doing two things. Firstly, by believing that I can get through it. If you don't believe in yourself, the fight is half lost already. Secondly, to accept the things I cannot control & choose how I'll face it. The latter is definitely more difficult for me, especially over the past few days.

The fantastic new flap on my leg started to show some worrisome signs and a dark spot also showed up on my stump end. I wasn't really concerned about my arm but thoughts of the leg flap rejecting once again terrified me. "What if …" lingered like a grey cloud in my head. I was helpless, as was my family, because there was nothing we could do but wait and see what happened & hope for the best. It was out of our control. But, even though the cloud remained in my head (I can't make the sun shine despite what some people think), I chose not to dwell on that cloud. I chose to surround myself with loving friends & family and to smile as much as I could smile & laugh as much as I could laugh.

I can't say my flap is looking better yet, but it's not any worse. More importantly, my doctor gave me the thumbs up today, saying it appears to be A-ok. Whew.

Another lucky break? Well that's part of my outlook … but that's only a matter of perspective, right?

How do you look at life? Are you feeling lucky?

Categories: Uncategorized | 4 Comments

Roomie Pool

Posted on March 5, 2012 by Nicole Moore

For those of you in the roomie pool, I said good bye to another roommate yesterday & hello to a new one. As expected, the turnover here is incredible. That makes 4 roommates for my current room plus 1 roommate from my other room for a total of 5. I'm guessing that this roomie will be around for a bit. We'll see who gets out first. ☺

Categories: Uncategorized | 1 Comment

Beautiful Day

Posted on March 7, 2012 by Nicole Moore

Wow!! Were we ever blessed with a beautiful day. Days like today are capable of renewing our spirits, making it possible to endure what little bit of winter that we may have left.

I was able to get up to a wheelchair today, wheel outside and spend some quality time with my father. What a nice day.

I have been standing (although not completely upright yet) and pivoting into my chair. The arterial grafts they made for my flaps have been tested over the past two days & so far, so good. Everything else also seems to be healing well. As a result, I have been given the go ahead to try walking tomorrow. Now don't go getting too excited as I'm not walking any marathons. Just a couple of steps with a crutch, but it's worth a lot to me. It means I'm one step closer to the door. One step closer to home and my kids, but shhh. We haven't told them yet. ☺

I hope everyone got to enjoy something about today.

Categories: Uncategorized | 2 Comments

On My Way...

Posted on March 8, 2012 by Nicole Moore

I did it!!!

Today I was able to walk with my crutch ... twice. It hurt like heck but I loved it. It's so nice to get off my bottom for the first time in 16 days. I haven't seen myself in the mirror yet but I'm convinced that my hips must be bigger due to my butt being flattened & squished out to the sides. ;)

So ... it's official. I'm going home tomorrow.

Yay!!!!!

I can't wait to tell the kids.

My leg is still immobilized & I'll still be on bedrest for the next 2 weeks but I truly believe that people heal better at home. The care here was once again, over the top, but how can they compete with my 2 little nurses I have awaiting at home?

Wish me luck & I'll keep you posted.

Categories: Uncategorized | 9 Comments

Through the Doors and Into a Whole New World

Posted on March 11, 2012 by Nicole Moore

As everyone knows by now, every day since I was re-admitted to the hospital, I was looking forward to the day I could go home.

When I was able to start walking or wheeling out of my room, the first thing I would do is look toward the exit doors and head in that direction. Some of the nurses would joke that they have to keep an eye on me or else I might just disappear. It was a good thing that my room was at the other end of the exit or I just might have.

The night before my discharge, a friend of mine text me saying "I bet you're already packed up." To which I responded back "already started sending stuff home yesterday." ☺

So needless to say, when discharge day came on Friday, I was up early & with the help of super nurse Erin, showered before breakfast & raring to go. I just had to wait for my ride who was delayed due to a snow storm??? What was with the weird weather of Friday?

I truly was saddened to say good bye to my roomie who, by the way, never changed so the roomie pool final number was 5. I wish her a quick recovery so she too can move onto real food instead of the hospital muck they serve. I was also sad to say bye to my surgical team and all of the wonderful staff on C5, especially Hasumie, Jay, Erin & Kelly, but nevertheless, elated to be leaving. Last year, round about the same time in fact, I left C5, but this time was a totally different feeling. You see, when I went home last year, I was incredibly happy, especially after such a traumatic absence but I always knew I'd have to return to retry the surgery. The knowledge that I'd have to rehabilitate only to come back lingered like heavy clouds that prevent you from summiting after finally climbing to the top camp on Mt. Everest. This time, with the success of these surgeries behind me, the clouds are gone. I left through those doors at Sunnybrook on Friday morning & went into a whole new world. A world with less burden & far more peace & tranquility. On this, exceptionally beautiful and springlike day, I wish you all a peaceful and happy day.

Categories: Uncategorized | 6 Comments

Alternate Contact Info

Posted on November 19, 2012 by Nicole Moore

Hi long lost world of bloggers.

For those that have been following my blog & wondering how I have been doing for the past 8 months, my apologies for not writing. It has been a long recovery this time around but I am doing well & keeping busy. If anyone is interested in knowing more, contact me. I will then try to create a blog entry covering the past 8 months.

To contact me, you will need to use my personal e-mail, not the blog site. I am still having several issues with my blog service provider. For the past 8 months I have been & am still unable to receive comments & e-mails via my blog page. If you have been sending messages but they have gone unanswered, it's not because I'm ignoring them. It's because I never got them.

All of your messages are important to me so please feel free to contact me at nlm472@gmail.com.

I am in the process of developing a Facebook page & hope to have it up & running soon hoping to make it easier for people.

I will post any changes.

Categories: Uncategorized | 0 Comments

"I Escaped Jaws"... Well Almost

Posted on August 5, 2013 by Nicole Moore

Well ... My notorious story made it on Discovery Channel's popular Shark Week.

My story along with other shark attack survivors will be on an episode called "I Escaped Jaws" on Tuesday August 6th at 9/8c. Very dramatic title!!

Tough initiation but I'm pretty excited to see the show. I hope they don't just spin the sensationalism of the story and portray sharks as demons. I hope they mention some of the positive messages I try to emit & promote shark conservation.

Life has been crazy busy with my recovery, TV & radio interviews, a book in the making, speaking internationally about my story, returning to work at the hospital ... yes still as an RN that people often exclaim when seeing me "hey, it's that shark lady!" (I'm ok with that) and of course spending time with my wonderful family.

My life is different now & has its challenges but I am still grateful for the beautiful life I have.

For those of you that have been waiting for a post & wondering what I've been up to, check out the episode.

http://dsc.discovery.com/tv-shows/shark-week

Live a life worth living. We all make a difference in the world.

Categories: Uncategorized | 0 Comments

Acknowledgements

This book would not be possible without our mutual friend Sharon Walton, who connected us suggesting, "You two will get along so well. Together, you can tell this story that so needs to be told." She was right and we tip our hats to you, Sharon, for knowing when the time was right to make the introduction.

Our thanks to George H. Burgess (www.flmnh.ufl.edu/fish/sharks) for sharing with us what factors can provoke shark attacks. We also recognize the astuteness of Dr. Gregory Skomal, one of the world's foremost experts on sharks, and thank him for his insights. His publication, *The Shark Handbook*, is full of fascinating details. We'd also like to thank the "shark lady," ninety-three-year-old Dr. Eugenie Clark, who gave us a deeper understanding of these fascinating animals and enlightened us with her years of research before she died.

Jim Toomey was very gracious in setting aside the humour of "Sherman's Lagoon" to talk seriously with us about his work in helping to save the world's oceans.

Dr. Laura Snell is an incredibly busy medical practitioner who nonetheless made herself available to answer our questions and provide details about operations that are two or three years in the past... for her, virtually a lifetime ago.

Thanks also to Dr. Andrew Fagan, Hasumie Hosogoe, Jay Clavio, Paul Addlestone, and Clasien Carlsen, who took valuable time from their medical postings to recall the events of Nicole's struggle for survival.

We thank Roy Clark, not just for his heroic efforts on the beach that day, staunching Nicole's bleeding, but for having the presence of mind to write down his recollections. Also Carlos Da Silva, whose career managing hotels was assaulted by the events of January 31, 2011.

"Superman and his chicas" opened their hearts and their minds to explain their feelings leading up to the Cancún trip and how Nicole's life has inspired them since. We thank them for their loyal friendship.

Rick McHale and Ted Barris read early versions of our manuscript and provided both encouragement and ideas that made for a stronger story. Thanks, guys. Patrick Boyer also encouraged Dundurn president Kirk Howard to read the manuscript, which resulted in his offer to be our publisher.

Lastly, the authors acknowledge the patience and tolerance of their family members, who were too often asked to put aside their own agendas to allow for the efforts that writing a book of this nature demands. We couldn't have completed *Shark Assault: An Amazing Story of Survival* without your acceptance and encouragement. Thank you.

— Nicole Moore and Peter Jennings

Share Your Story

As rare as shark attacks are, we've received stories about other assaults since beginning this book. If you have an incident you'd like to share, please visit www.sharkassault.com. We may include your account in a future edition of *Shark Assault*.